·THE TASTE OF·
ITALY

PUBLISHING

Compiled by Frédéric Lebain and Jean-Paul Paireault
Photographed by Jean-Paul Paireault
Designed by Sally Strugnell and Alison Jewell
Adapted and Translated by Lynn Jennings-Collombet

Acknowledgments

The publishers would like to thank the following for their
valuable assistance and cooperation in the production of
this book:

Madame Bayle, at Mas Le Plan in Lourmarin, for facilities for
location photography.
The shopkeepers of Lourmarin and Pertuis for their special
efforts to obtain and provide a variety of fresh and attractive
fish, meats and general provisions.
Monsieur Thomas, Faïencerie de Gien, Djan d'Harfeuille in
Clamart, Morcrette, and Villeroy and Boch for the loan of
glassware and plates.
Cine Photo Provence, in Aix-en-Provence for film processing.
Kettie Artigaud for her help with general styling and furnishing.
Kathleen Jennings for her patience and help throughout the
adaptaion and translation of this book.
Monsieur Remande, director of l'Ecole Supérieure de Cuisine
in Paris.
Thanks are also due to Monsieur and Madame Lebain,
Monsieur David and Madame Marie-Solange Bezaunt,
Madame Chardot, and Monsieur Bernard Bouton of Sougé.

CLB 2195
This edition published in 1989 by CLB Publishing Inc,
Airport Business Center, 29 Kripes Road, East Granby, CT 06026.
© 1989 Colour Library Books Ltd., Godalming, Surrey, England.
Typesetting by Words and Spaces, Rowlands Castle, Hants, England.
Color separations by Hong Kong Graphic Arts Ltd., Hong Kong.
Produced in England.

ISBN 0 86283 754 5

· THE TASTE OF ·
ITALY

Frederic Lebain · Jean-Paul Paireault

Introduction

Italian cooking has changed considerably since Roman times, when banquets included sheep stuffed with oysters, and whole roast peacock, but food itself continues to be of the utmost importance. A meal is still very much a social occasion in Italy, providing the chance to gather friends and family around the same table.

Modern Italian cooking reflects all the warmth, vitality and charm of the country itself. Tradition is also important, though, thankfully, reverence for the past does not extend to reviving ancient banquet menus! In Italian kitchens, cooking has always been looked upon as a pleasure, not as a chore, and this attitude is still apparent today. Italians take food seriously, but think cooking and eating it should be fun, too.

All the traditional recipes are brought out for holidays, but even an everyday meal in Italy usually comprises three courses – a soup or pasta course, a main course and fruit. A more elaborate meal, for a large family gathering perhaps, begins with an antipasto, which means, literally, "before the pasta" and which is most often something simple, such as marinated vegetables or a selection of cheeses and cured meats. This is followed by either soup or pasta.

Vegetables are so highly prized in Italy that they are often served as a separate course, after the soup or pasta, to be enjoyed without the distraction of other food. Next comes the main course, of fish, meat or poultry, accompanied by polenta, risotto or potatoes and a salad. A sweet course, whether a rich dessert or simply fresh fruit, is served last.

Whether simple or sumptuous, Italian meals are based on whatever fresh, seasonal ingredients are available locally and, while pasta, pizza, shellfish and veal dishes, vegetable salads and ice cream desserts are characteristic of Italian cooking in general, regional differences make for infinite variety.

In Sicily, vegetable dishes and salads based on artichokes are common, as are veal and chicken dishes using Marsala, the delicious, sweet fortified wine made locally. Pasta served with a beautiful, green sauce based on fragrant basil leaves is the speciality of the area around Genoa. Milan is famous for a delicious risotto dish and Venice for a quickly cooked calf's liver recipe.

Any country with so many miles of coastline is bound to have a wealth of fish and seafood recipes in its culinary repertoire. Here are scampi, lobster, red mullet, sardines, silver bream, swordfish, squid, octopus – the list goes on and on. Grilled with herbs, garlic or lemon and drizzled with olive oil, even simply cooked fish tastes out of this world.

The Italian climate means a long growing season, so fruit trees flourish, as do grape vines. With fresh, local melons, figs, grapes, peaches, pears and blood oranges widely available, it's no wonder Italians favor fruit to end a meal. The only exception is in the north, where meals often end with a creamy pastry.

Yet, despite all the variety of Italian cuisine, it is of pizza and pasta that everyone thinks first when they think of Italian food. Undeniably tasty, these must be two of Italy's most famous exports.

Pizza originated in Naples. Bakers used to roll out their bread dough to make a thin base and cover it with simple toppings, such as olives, anchovies, mushrooms, cheese or onions. Tomatoes, now an indispensable part of a good pizza, were not even grown in Italy when the first pizzas were created. These first pizzas were baked in huge bread ovens, which stayed hot long after the day's bread was done. Just about every ingredient imaginable, some not even remotely Italian, has been used to top pizzas. However, a really delicious pizza is not a dumping ground for leftovers, but a careful selection of ingredients that complement one another.

Pasta used to mean either spaghetti with a meat sauce or macaroni with a cheese one. Our tastes have become more adventurous as we've discovered all the different pasta shapes and all the hundreds of sauce recipes, from simple cream and freshly grated Parmesan to complicated combinations that take hours to prepare and cook. Fortunately, fresh pasta is now available ready-made for real pasta lovers without either a machine or the time to make their own.

Whether traditionally robust or stylish and sophisticated, Italian cooking is always a celebration of the best food the land has to offer and of the talents of the cook who prepares it. Good Italian cooking is also as close as your own kitchen.

─── SERVES 4 ───

CABBAGE AND PASTA SOUP

Chicken stock flavored with bacon,
cabbage, pasta and garlic is the base
for this light and tasty appetizer.

Step 1

Step 1

Step 1

☐ 6 leaves white cabbage ☐ 1 cup small shell pasta
☐ 1 strip bacon, cut into small dice
☐ 1 clove garlic, chopped ☐ 1 tbsp olive oil
☐ 3 cups chicken stock ☐ Salt and pepper

1. Cut the cabbage into thin strips. To do this, roll the leaves into cigar shapes and cut with a very sharp knife.

2. Heat the olive oil and fry the garlic, bacon and cabbage together for 2 minutes.

3. Pour over the stock, season with salt and pepper and cook on a moderate heat for 30 minutes.

4. Add the pasta to the soup after it has been cooking for 15 minutes.

5. Check the seasoning and serve.

TIME Preparation takes about 5 minutes and cooking takes approximately 35 minutes.

SERVING IDEA Sprinkle over a little grated Parmesan cheese just before serving the soup.

VARIATION Leave the piece of bacon whole and remove before serving the soup.

☐

OPPOSITE

CABBAGE AND
PASTA SOUP

— SERVES 4 —

GNOCCHI WITH TOMATO SAUCE

*Coated in a tasty tomato sauce and sprinkled
with Parmesan cheese, the gnocchi are
crisped up under a hot broiler.*

Step 3

Step 4

Step 5

☐ 1lb potatoes, steamed in their jackets
☐ 1 cup all-purpose flour   ☐ 1 egg yolk
☐ 1 cup grated Parmesan cheese
☐ 6 tomatoes, peeled, seeded and roughly chopped
☐ 1 shallot, finely chopped ☐ 1 clove garlic, chopped
☐ 2 tbsps olive oil
☐ 1 bouquet garni, made up with parsley, thyme and 1 bay leaf
☐ Salt and pepper

1. Peel the potatoes and push them though a fine sieve.

2. Beat the flour and egg yolk into the potato. Stir in ¼ cup Parmesan cheese and season with salt and pepper.

3. Place this gnocchi dough into a pastry bag with a wide, plain tube.

4. Bring to the boil a large saucepan of salted water. Once the water is boiling, hold the bag over the pan and squeeze out balls of dough, detaching the dough from the tube with the sharp downward movement of a knife.

5. Remove the gnocchi as they rise to the surface and drain them on a tea towel.

6. Heat the oil in a frying pan and gently fry the shallot and garlic, then add the tomato, bouquet garni, salt and pepper for approximately 15 minutes.

7. The sauce should be quite liquid after 15 minutes. Remove the bouquet garni, place the sauce in a liquidizer and blend smooth.

8. Put the sauce back over a gentle heat, add the gnochi and heat through.

9. Tip into an ovenproof dish and top with the remaining Parmesan cheese. Crisp up under a hot broiler and serve.

TIME   Preparation takes about 40 minutes and cooking takes approximately 40 minutes.

VARIATION   Use Mozzarella cheese for the topping instead of the remaining Parmesan; this will give a slightly milder flavor to the dish.

COOK'S TIP   Gnocchi dough should be used as soon as it is made as it tends to get sticky if left.

☐

OPPOSITE

GNOCCHI WITH
TOMATO SAUCE

———— SERVES 4 ————

SPRATS IN MAYONNAISE

Step 1

Step 3

☐ 1¼ lbs sprats   ☐ 1 carrot   ☐ 1 sprig rosemary
☐ Small bunch parsley   ☐ 1 bay leaf   ☐ 1 egg yolk
☐ 1 tsp mustard   ☐ 1 clove garlic, chopped
☐ Salt and pepper   ☐ ½ cup olive oil

1. Make a vegetable stock by boiling together in a large saucepan of water the carrot, rosemary, parsley and the bay leaf. Season well with salt and pepper and simmer gently until the liquid is well flavored.

2. Strain the stock into a clean saucepan through a fine sieve.

3. Bring the stock to a gentle simmer and add the fish. Cook for approximately 2 minutes (longer if you prefer your fish very well cooked). Drain and set the fish aside to cool.

4. To make the mayonnaise, beat together the egg yolk, mustard, salt, pepper and garlic, then add the olive oil drop by drop, beating continuously.

5. Serve the fish hot or cold with the mayonnaise.

TIME   The stock can be prepared in advance and kept in the fridge. If the stock has been made in advance, cooking time is reduced to a few minutes. Preparation of the mayonnaise takes about 5 minutes.

SERVING IDEA   Serve on a bed of mixed lettuce, well washed, dried and broken into manageable pieces.

WATCHPOINT   It is important to add the olive oil a little at a time, so that the mayonnaise will be very firm.

☐

OPPOSITE

SPRATS IN
MAYONNAISE

——— SERVES 4 ———

TOMATO AND MOZZARELLA

*The classic summer appetizer to almost every family meal
in Italy. Use large, juicy tomatoes, fresh basil, moist
Mozzarella and the finest olive oil you can buy.*

Step 1

Step 1

☐ 4 large tomatoes   ☐ 1 Mozzarella cheese
☐ 1 tbsp wine vinegar   ☐ 3 tbsps olive oil
☐ 10 fresh basil leaves   ☐ Salt and pepper

1. Cut the Mozzarella cheese into rounds. Then, using a pastry cutter, trim the rounds into neat, decorative shapes.

2. Place the tomatoes stalk side down and cut downwards into about 4 slices, but do not cut through all the way to the bottom.

3. Ease a slice of cheese into each of the 4 cuts and repeat on each tomato.

4. Cut the basil leaves lengthwise into thin strips and mix into the vinegar and the olive oil.

5. Season the sauce to taste with salt and pepper and pour over each tomato before serving.

TIME   Preparation takes about 15 minutes.

COOK'S TIP   Use a sharp, finely serrated knife to cut the cheese. Do not push down hard, but use a sawing action; this will keep the slices in one piece.

LEFTOVERS   Use the Mozzarella trimmings on a pizza, or chop into small cubes and add to a tossed salad.

☐

OPPOSITE

TOMATO AND
MOZZARELLA

—— SERVES 4 ——

RAVIOLI SOUP

*Fresh pasta rectangles are filled with Parma ham
and butter, then cooked in chicken stock. A tasty
and filling appetizer for that extra special meal.*

Step 1

Step 2

Step 3

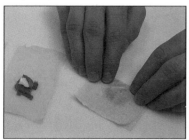

Step 4

□ 8oz pasta dough
□ 3 slices Parma ham, cut into very thin strips
□ 4 cups chicken stock □ 2 tbsps butter
□ 1 egg, beaten
□ 1 sprig tarragon, leaves stripped off and cut into thin strips
□ 2 tbsps light cream □ Nutmeg □ Salt and pepper

1. Roll the pasta dough very thinly, either with a rolling pin or by passing through a pasta machine, and cut it into rectangles.

2. Place a little Parma ham and butter on one half of each rectangle.

3. Brush the edges of each piece of dough with the beaten egg.

4. Fold each rectangle in half to form a square and pinch the edges well with your fingers to seal. Either trim these squares into various shapes or decorate the edges of the squares with the prongs of a fork.

5. Bring the stock to the boil, and season with nutmeg, salt and pepper.

6. Tip the ravioli into the stock and cook for approximately 2 to 5 minutes, depending on the thickness of the ravioli.

7. Stir the cream into the soup just before serving and sprinkle over the tarragon. Serve hot.

TIME   Preparation takes about 40 minutes (if you have just made the pasta dough, it should rest for 30 minutes in the fridge before rolling) and cooking time is approximately 10 minutes.

COOK'S TIP   The use of cream in the soup is optional, but it gives a nice smooth taste to the stock.

WATCHPOINT   The cooking of the ravioli in the soup should be done on a very gentle simmer – the ravioli may burst open if soup boils vigorously.

□

OPPOSITE

RAVIOLI SOUP

─── SERVES 4 ───

MACARONI WITH OLIVE SAUCE

*Macaroni is served here with butter, garlic
and finely chopped olives. A very tasty
dish that makes an ideal appetizer.*

Step 2

Step 2

☐ ¾ lb macaroni
☐ 10 olives, green and/or black, finely chopped
☐ 1 clove garlic, finely chopped ☐ ¼ cup butter
☐ Salt and pepper

1. Cook the macaroni to your liking in salted, boiling water. Rinse in hot water and set aside to drain.

2. Melt the butter in a saucepan and add the garlic and olives. Cook for 1 minute and then stir in the macaroni.

3. Check the seasoning, adding salt and pepper as necessary. Serve hot.

TIME   Preparation takes about 10 minutes and cooking time is approximately 20 minutes.

VARIATION   Add a few chopped capers to the olives, but go easy on the seasoning with salt.

COOK'S TIP   Rinse the macaroni really well under hot water to prevent it from sticking together.

☐

OPPOSITE

MACARONI WITH
OLIVE SAUCE

SAUTEED GNOCCHI
WITH FRESH BASIL

*Classically cooked gnocchi are sautéed in butter,
garlic and freshly sliced basil. They turn a
lovely golden brown and are quite delicious.*

Step 1

Step 2

Step 2

☐ 1lb potatoes, steamed in their skins   ☐ 1 egg yolk
☐ 1 cup all-purpose flour, sifted
☐ 2 tbsps grated Parmesan cheese   ☐ 1 clove garlic, chopped
☐ 10 basil leaves, cut into very thin slices   ☐ ¼ cup butter
☐ Pinch nutmeg   ☐ Salt and pepper

1. Peel the potatoes and push them through a fine sieve.

2. Beat the egg yolk and the flour into the potato purée. Season with the nutmeg, salt and pepper. Stir in the grated Parmesan cheese.

3. Bring a large quantity of salted water to the boil.

4. Place the gnocchi dough in a pastry bag fitted with a wide, plain tube. Hold the tube over the water and squeeze the dough out into small balls.

5. Remove the gnocchi with a slotted spoon as they rise to the surface, and leave on a tea towel to drain.

6. Once all the gnocchi are cooked, melt the butter in a frying pan, add the garlic and the basil and fry for 1 minute.

7. Add the gnocchi and sauté, shaking the pan frequently until the gnocchi are golden brown all over. Serve immediately.

TIME   Preparation takes about 40 minutes and cooking takes approximately 30 minutes.

VARIATION   For extra flavor, add a little extra basil, finely chopped, to the gnocchi dough

COOK'S TIP   Cook the gnocchi in batches, allowing one batch to finish cooking before adding another.

☐

OPPOSITE

SAUTEED
GNOCCHI WITH
FRESH BASIL

─── SERVES 4 ───

FRIED LANGOUSTINE

*Deep-fried langoustines served with home-made
mayonnaise flavored with garlic and
fresh basil – a delicious appetizer.*

Step 1

Step 1

☐ 20 small langoustines   ☐ Flour for dredging   ☐ 1 egg yolk
☐ ½ tsp mustard   ☐ 5 fresh basil leaves, finely chopped
☐ 1 cup olive oil   ☐ 1 clove garlic, finely chopped
☐ 1 lemon   ☐ 1 egg   ☐ Salt and pepper   ☐ Oil for deep frying

1. Remove the heads and peel the langoustines.

2. Season with salt and pepper and then dredge them in the flour. Shake to remove excess flour.

3. Beat together the egg yolk, mustard, salt, pepper and fresh basil. Add the olive oil in a thin, steady trickle, whisking continuously until a thick mayonnaise is obtained.

4. Stir into the mayonnaise the finely chopped garlic.

5. Peel the lemon, separate the segments and remove the membrane. Cut the flesh into tiny pieces and set aside.

6. Heat the oil to 350°F. Beat the egg and briefly dip the langoustines into it. Place the langoustines in the hot oil and fry until crisp and golden. Drain on paper towels and serve with a little lemon and the mayonnaise.

TIME   Preparation takes about 25 minutes and cooking takes approximately 5 to 10 minutes, depending on the number of batches you fry the langoustines in.

VARIATION   Other ingredients such as chopped capers and finely diced onion can be added to the mayonnaise.

COOK'S TIP   To prevent the langoustines from sticking together, fry them 1 or 2 at a time; more can be cooked together if the pan is very large.

☐

OPPOSITE

FRIED
LANGOUSTINE

—— SERVES 4 ——

CARPACCIO WITH HERBS

*Thin slices of fresh beef make a marvelous
starter to even the most refined dinner party.*

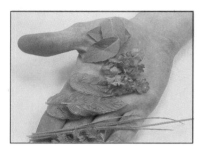

Step 2

☐ 1lb fresh fillet steak ☐ 4 basil leaves ☐ 5 chive leaves
☐ ½ tsp coriander ☐ 3 mint leaves
☐ ½ tsp chopped parsley
☐ 1 onion, cut into very thin slices ☐ 2 tbsps olive oil
☐ Squeeze lemon juice ☐ Salt and pepper

1. Slice the meat thinly and arrange on a serving plate.

2. Chop all the herbs together as finely as possible and stir them into the olive oil.

3. Add a squeeze of lemon juice to the oil and herb mixture and brush the sauce all over the slices of beef.

4. Scatter over the slices of onion and serve.

TIME   Preparation takes about 40 minutes.

COOK'S TIP   Place the meat in the freezer for 1-2 hours; this will make it easier to slice thinly.

WATCHPOINT   The carpaccio must be prepared and eaten the same day.

☐

OPPOSITE

CARPACCIO
WITH HERBS

MILANESE VEGETABLE SOUP

*Small cubes of vegetables cooked in a
chicken stock with a little smoked bacon
make for a delicious soup.*

Step 2

☐ 4 cups chicken stock   ☐ 1 chard leaf   ☐ ½ carrot
☐ ½ eggplant   ☐ ½ zucchini   ☐ 1 onion
☐ 1 stick celery   ☐ 10 basil leaves
☐ 2 strips bacon   ☐ Salt and pepper

1. If using freshly made stock, carefully filter it through a fine cheesecloth and then pour it into a saucepan and bring to the boil

2. Cut all the vegetables (not the basil) and the bacon into small cubes.

3. Add the vegetables to the stock and simmer gently for 15 minutes.

4. Add the bacon cubes to the soup for the last 8 minutes of cooking time.

5. Check the seasoning and add salt and pepper as necessary.

6. Cut the basil leaves into thin strips and add these to the soup just before serving.

TIME   Preparation takes about 25 minutes and cooking takes approximately 20 minutes.

VARIATION   Add any other vegetables you have to this soup; they can only enhance it.

COOK'S TIP   Check the seasoning when the soup is cooked, as the bacon tends to give a rather salty taste. Add salt sparingly, but plenty of pepper will do no harm.

☐

OPPOSITE

MILANESE
VEGETABLE SOUP

CHICKPEA SALAD

Squid and chick peas
in garlic and shallot sauce –
a simple but original appetizer.

Step 1

Step 2

☐ 2 cups chickpeas	☐ 1 carrot, cut into 4
☐ 1 onion stuck with 2 cloves	☐ Sprig thyme ☐ 1 bay leaf
☐ 2 squid, washed and emptied	
☐ 1 tbsp chopped parsley	☐ 1 clove garlic, chopped
☐ 1 shallot, chopped	☐ 1 tbsp wine vinegar
☐ 3 tbsps olive oil	☐ Salt and pepper

1. Soak the chickpeas overnight in plenty of cold water.

2. Drain the peas and cook them in salted, boiling water with the carrot, onion, thyme and the bay leaf. Cook for about 2 hours, depending on how you prefer your chickpeas

3. Cook the prepared squid in a steamer for approximately 4 minutes.

4. Cut the cooked squid into thin rounds.

5. Make the sauce by mixing together the salt, pepper, vinegar, shallot, garlic, parsley and the olive oil.

6. When the peas are cooked through, remove the onion, carrot, bay leaf and thyme and discard. Rinse the peas in cold water and set aside to drain.

7. Once the peas are cold, combine them with the squid and the sauce. Serve at room temperature on small individual plates.

TIME   Preparation takes about 10 minutes, plus overnight soaking for the peas, and total cooking time is approximately 2 hours and 10 minutes.

VARIATION   Any member of the squid family could be used in this recipe.

WATCHPOINT   It is essential to soak the chickpeas overnight, otherwise cooking will take much longer.

☐

OPPOSITE

CHICKPEA SALAD

—— SERVES 4 ——

LIVORNESE FISH SOUP

A very tasty, slightly spicy
fish soup. Great for
cold winter evenings.

Step 2

Step 3

Step 5

□ 3 ½ lbs fish (small whole fish and a little shellfish)
□ 1 onion, sliced   □ 1 carrot, sliced
□ Small bunch parsley, well rinsed and dried
□ 1 small chili pepper, chopped (discard the seeds)
□ 3 cloves garlic   □ ½ cup white wine
□ 4 tomatoes, quartered   □ 1 stick French bread
□ 3 tbsps olive oil
□ ½ cup finely grated Parmesan cheese   □ Salt and pepper

1. Clean, gut and rinse the fish and shellfish well.

2. Heat the olive oil in a large pan and gently fry the carrots, onion, chili pepper and the parsley.

3. Add the fish and shellfish and continue frying for 4 minutes.

4. Deglaze the pan with the dry white wine and then stir in the garlic and the tomatoes.

5. Stir well and continue cooking for a few minutes, then pour over plenty of water. Bring to the boil, reduce the heat and simmer gently for 1 hour.

6. Taste the soup and adjust seasoning as necessary.

7. Cut the French stick into slices and toast them under the broiler.

8. Strain the soup through a fine sieve, pressing the fish well.

9. Serve the soup piping hot spooned over the toast and sprinkled with the grated Parmesan cheese.

TIME   Preparation takes about 15 minutes and total cooking time is approximately 1 hour and 30 minutes.

COOK'S TIP   Use small sea fish for this recipe; they are much richer in flavor. Add a few small crabs and some shellfish.

□

OPPOSITE

LIVORNESE FISH
SOUP

——— SERVES 4 ———

CRISP-FRIED SPRATS

*Coated in flour and crisply fried in hot oil,
these sprats make a delicious appetizer.*

Step 4

Step 5

☐ 1¼ lbs sprats   ☐ 1½ cups all-purpose flour   ☐ 2 lemons
☐ Salt and pepper   ☐ Oil for deep frying

1. Wash the fish well in plenty of cold water.
2. Dry them on tea towels – the fish must be completely dry.
3. Heat the oil to 350°F.
4. Toss the fish in the flour and then shake off any excess.
5. Lower the fish into the hot oil and fry until crisp and golden.
6. Drain on paper towels and serve with lemon rounds, salt and pepper.

TIME   Preparation takes about 10 minutes and cooking takes approximately 20 minutes (depending on the number of batches you are cooking).

SERVING IDEA   Serve fried sprats as an appetizer on a bed of lettuce together with fresh mayonnaise.

WATCHPOINT   Sprats do not usually have to be emptied, although this is advisable with larger ones, as these may have too strong a taste.

☐

OPPOSITE

CRISP-FRIED
SPRATS

——— SERVES 4 ———

CARPACCIO WITH CAPERS

Capers and fresh beef – an amazing combination.

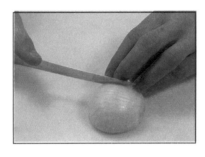

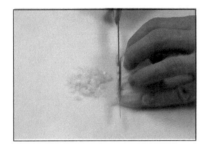

☐ 1lb fillet steak   ☐ 1 onion, chopped
☐ 2 tbsps capers   ☐ 2 tbsps olive oil
☐ 1 squeeze lemon juice   ☐ Salt and pepper

1. Cut the beef into very thin slices, and spread them out onto a serving plate.

2. Mix together the oil, lemon juice and the capers.

3. Season the beef with plenty of pepper and a little salt.

4. Sprinkle over the onion and then pour the sauce all over the beef.

5. Allow to marinate for at least 10 minutes before serving. Serve at room temperature.

TIME   Preparation takes about 30 minutes.

VARIATION   A little of the vinegar from the jar of capers may be used to replace the lemon juice in this recipe.

WATCHPOINT   It is very important to use finest quality, tender beef for this recipe. A cut from the center of the fillet is best.

☐

OPPOSITE

CARPACCIO
WITH CAPERS

——— SERVES 4 ———

TARRAGON OMELET

*A tarragon-flavored omelet
accompanied by a tossed mixed salad
makes a good, quick evening meal.*

Step 1

Step 2

□ 8 eggs   □ 1 sprig fresh tarragon
□ 1 tbsp oil   □ 2 tbsps heavy cream   □ Salt and pepper

---

1. Remove the leaves from the sprig of tarragon and cut them lengthwise into thin strips.
2. Beat together the eggs, tarragon and cream.
3. Season with plenty of salt and pepper.
4. Heat the oil in a frying pan, pour in the omelet mixture and cook until golden on the bottom.
5. Roll the omelet up and serve on a heated plate.

TIME   Preparation and cooking take about 15 minutes.

VARIATION   Use dried tarragon or tarragon conserved in vinegar to replace fresh tarragon.

WATCHPOINT   The oil should be hot when you pour in the omelet mixture. Using a non-stick pan makes rolling the omelet easier.

□

OPPOSITE

TARRAGON
OMELET

—— SERVES 4 ——

CHEESE FONDUE

A tasty and ever-popular party snack.

Step 3

Step 3

☐ 1lb Fontina cheese ☐ 3 tbsps chopped chives
☐ 3 egg yolks ☐ 2 tbsps butter ☐ 4 slices white bread
☐ 2 cups milk ☐ 2 tbsps oil ☐ Salt and pepper

1. The day before serving the fondue, cut the cheese into small cubes, place in a bowl and pour over the milk to cover (add more milk if required). Leave to soak overnight in a cool place.

2. The next day, cut the bread into small cubes and fry in the hot oil.

3. About 10 minutes before serving the fondue, pour the cheese and milk mixture into a flameproof casserole, beat in the egg yolks and the butter and beat over a gentle heat until the cheese melts.

4. Season with salt and pepper and serve immediately, for the guests to dip the cubes of bread into the mixture on long-handled fondue forks.

5. Serve little plates of chopped chives around the table; guests can then dip the hot, cheese covered cubes in the chives.

TIME Overnight soak, 20 minutes preparation and approximately 10 minutes cooking time.

VARIATION Other herbs, such as tarragon, can be served with the fondue.

WATCHPOINT Don't worry if the cheese forms a hard mass during cooking; it will melt eventually.

☐

OPPOSITE

CHEESE FONDUE

—— SERVES 4 ——

PARMESAN SOUFFLE OMELET

*A light and puffy omelet flavored with
fresh, chopped chives and Parmesan cheese.*

Step 1

Step 2

☐ 8 eggs, separated   ☐ ½ cup Parmesan cheese, grated
☐ ½ cup milk   ☐ 2 tbsps chopped chives
☐ 1 tbsp oil   ☐ 2 tbsps butter   ☐ Salt and pepper

1. Mix the egg yolks into the milk with the Parmesan, chives, salt and pepper.

2. Whisk the whites until very stiff and then gently incorporate the yolks into the whites.

3. Heat the oil and the butter in a large frying pan and cook both sides of the omelet until golden brown. Serve immediately.

TIME   Preparation takes about 15 minutes and cooking takes approximately 10 to 15 minutes.

VARIATION   Try different fresh, chopped herbs in this omelet.

COOK'S TIP   Turning a large omelet like this one can be quite a difficult task. As an alternative, use a small frying pan and cook individual omelets for your guests, keeping the first ones warm in an open oven.

☐

OPPOSITE

PARMESAN
SOUFFLE OMELET

— SERVES 4 —

POACHED EGGS IN BAROLO SAUCE

*Poached eggs served with an unusual
red wine sauce flavored with shallots,
mushrooms and chicken stock.*

Step 7

Step 7

Step 8

☐ 4 eggs ☐ 2 thick strips bacon, cut into small cubes
☐ 2 cups Barolo wine ☐ 2 shallots, finely chopped
☐ 4 slices white bread ☐ 1 cup chicken stock
☐ 3 large mushrooms, finely sliced ☐ ¼ cup butter
☐ 1 tbsp wine vinegar ☐ Salt and pepper

1. Place the wine, shallots and mushrooms in a pan and reduce by ¾ over a high heat.

2. Stir the chicken stock into the reduced wine sauce and reduce by half over a high heat.

3. Cut the slices of bread into either small rounds or squares and toast them under a hot broiler. Set aside.

4. Strain the reduced sauce through a very fine sieve into a clean saucepan.

5. Add the bacon to the saucepan and set it on a moderate heat. Continue to cook for a further 3 minutes.

6. When the 3 minutes are up, whisk in small pieces of the butter until it is used up. Remove from direct heat, but keep warm.

7. Poach the eggs in boiling water to which you have added the vinegar and a little salt.

8. Drain the eggs once they are cooked (between 2 to 4 minutes) on a clean tea towel and set on a serving plate.

9. Serve the eggs on the toasts with the sauce poured over.

TIME   Preparation takes about 20 minutes and cooking takes approximately 40 minutes.

VARIATION   If Barolo is not available, use any other dry red wine.

WATCHPOINT   If you like your poached eggs very soft, take particular care when drying them on the tea towel.

☐

OPPOSITE

POACHED EGGS IN
BAROLO SAUCE

—— SERVES 4 ——

WILD MUSHROOM PIZZA

This recipe shows how to make the bread dough, necessary for all the pizza recipes. The pizza is coated with tomato sauce and wild mushrooms.

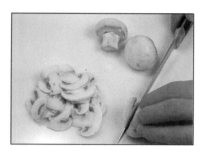

Step 4

BREAD DOUGH

☐ 2 ¼ cups flour, sifted   ☐ ½ cup tepid water
☐ ¼ cup milk   ☐ 1 tbsp yeast   ☐ Pinch salt

TOPPING

☐ 1 quantity tomato sauce (see Mozzarella Pizza recipe)
☐ ¼ cup butter   ☐ 1 shallot, finely chopped
☐ 4 button mushrooms, finely sliced
☐ 1 cup wild mushrooms, finely sliced
☐ ½ clove garlic, finely chopped   ☐ 20 olives
☐ 2 tbsps grated Parmesan cheese   ☐ Salt and pepper

1. Mix the yeast, water and milk together in a small bowl. Stir until the yeast dissolves.

2. Place the flour in a large bowl, add the pinch of salt and then mix in the yeast mixture. Knead the dough by hand for 3 minutes.

3. Cover with a tea towel and leave to rise in a warm place for 45 minutes.

4. Heat the butter and fry the shallot, mushrooms and garlic for 2 minutes.

5. Roll out the dough on a floured surface into the desired thickness and shape.

6. Spread the tomato sauce evenly over the pizza dough.

7. Place the mushrooms on the sauce and then sprinkle over the grated Parmesan cheese.

8. Dot the olives over the pizza and season with salt and pepper.

9. Cook in a very hot oven until the dough base is crisp and golden brown. Serve immediately.

TIME   Preparation takes about 30 minutes, rising time for the dough is 45 minutes and cooking takes approximately 30 minutes in all.

COOK'S TIP   The oven should be preheated to a very high temperature so that the pizza cooks quickly and is nice and crisp.

TIME SAVER   Frozen pizza dough can be used as a quick alternative.

☐

OPPOSITE

WILD MUSHROOM
PIZZA

—— SERVES 4 ——

MOZZARELLA PIZZA

*The recipe for this quick and easy pizza
shows how to make the tomato sauce
that is common to all the pizza recipes.*

Step 1

Step 1

Step 1

☐ 1 quantity bread dough (see Wild Mushroom Pizza recipe)
☐ ½ onion, finely sliced   ☐ 7oz Mozzarella cheese
☐ 2 tomatoes, sliced   ☐ 2 slices ham, cut into small pieces
☐ 1 tsp marjoram   ☐ Salt and pepper

TOMATO SAUCE

☐ 4 large tomatoes, seeded, peeled and crushed
☐ 1 onion, finely chopped   ☐ 1 bay leaf
☐ A few drops Tabasco sauce   ☐ 1 small sprig thyme
☐ 1 clove garlic, finely chopped   ☐ 2 tbsp olive oil
☐ Salt and pepper.

1. To make the tomato sauce, heat the olive oil in a frying pan and fry the onion. Then add the tomato, bay leaf, thyme, Tabasco and garlic. Season with salt and pepper and cook for approximately 30 minutes. Stir frequently.

2. Once the liquid from the tomatoes has almost evaporated, remove the bay leaf and the sprig of thyme. Allow the sauce to cool somewhat and then blend smooth in a food processor.

3. Roll the dough out into a round and spread with the prepared tomato sauce.

4. Lay the sliced tomato over the tomato sauce, then the onion and the ham.

5. Cut the Mozzarella into thin slices and lay the slices on the pizza. Season with salt and pepper and sprinkle over the marjoram.

6. Cook in a very hot oven for approximately 15 minutes and serve immediately.

TIME   Preparation takes about 20 minutes and cooking takes approximately 45 minutes.

VARIATION   Sprinkle the pizza with fresh, chopped herbs such as parsley or tarragon just before baking.

WATCHPOINT   Remember to remove the bay leaf and the sprig of thyme before blending the sauce in the food processor, otherwise the sauce will have too strong a flavor.

☐

OPPOSITE

MOZZARELLA
PIZZA

—— SERVES 4 ——

ONION PIZZA

*Tasty pizzas coated in tomato sauce,
with anchovies and lots of sliced onion.*

Step 1

☐ 1 quantity bread dough (see Wild Mushroom Pizza recipe)
☐ 1 quantity tomato sauce (see Mozzarella Pizza recipe)
☐ 2 large onions, thinly sliced   ☐ 16 anchovy tenderloins
☐ 1 tsp dried onion   ☐ Salt and pepper

1. Roll the dough out into two rounds.

2. Spread the tomato sauce evenly over the two pizzas.

3. Place the sliced onion over the sauce and lay the anchovy tenderloins neatly over the onion.

4. Season with salt and pepper. Sprinkle over the dried onion and cook in a very hot oven for approximately 20 minutes, or until crisp and cooked. Serve immediately.

TIME   Preparation takes about 20 minutes and cooking takes 20 minutes.

SERVING IDEA   As you serve the pizzas, sprinkle over a little hot peppered olive oil. Alternatively, add a drop or two of Tabasco to the tomato sauce.

COOK'S TIP   To allow for the elasticity of the dough, roll the rounds larger than desired and leave them for a minute to settle before spreading over the tomato sauce.

☐

OPPOSITE

ONION PIZZA

―――― SERVES 4 ――――

SOUFFLE PIZZA WITH CHEESE

*A puffy half-moon pizza, great
for an evening meal with friends,
served with a tossed green salad.*

Step 2

Step 5

Step 5

☐ 1 quantity bread dough (see Wild Mushroom Pizza recipe)
☐ ½ quantity tomato sauce (see Mozzarella Pizza recipe)
☐ 2 small goat cheeses   ☐ 1 tsp marjoram
☐ 1 large onion, chopped   ☐ 1 egg   ☐ 1 tbsp olive oil
☐ Salt and pepper

1. Roll the dough out into a round on a lightly floured surface.

2. Pour the tomato sauce over half of the round and sprinkle over the onion.

3. Break the cheese into small pieces and scatter over the onion.

4. Season with salt and pepper and sprinkle with the marjoram and the olive oil.

5. Beat the egg and brush over the edges of the dough. Fold one half of the round over the other half to form a half-moon shape. Press down well along the edges to seal.

6. Cook in a very hot oven and remove when the pizza is lightly colored on the surface. Serve immediately.

TIME   Preparation takes about 25 minutes and cooking takes approximately 15 minutes.

SERVING IDEA   Serve this type of pizza with a mixed green salad.

VARIATION   Replace the olive oil with peppered oil to enliven the flavors a little.

☐

OPPOSITE

SOUFFLE PIZZA
WITH CHEESE

---- SERVES 4 ----

PEPPER PIZZA

*Three different types of peppers, slices of
Mozzarella cheese, and tomato are combined
in a mouthwatering vegetarian pizza.*

Step 2

Step 3

Step 4

☐ 1 quantity bread dough (see Wild Mushroom Pizza recipe)
☐ 1 quantity tomato sauce (see Mozzarella Pizza recipe)
☐ 1 red pepper, seeded and cut into thin slices
☐ 1 green pepper, seeded and cut into thin slices
☐ 1 yellow pepper, seeded and cut into thin slices
☐ 7oz Mozzarella cheese   ☐ 1 tsp marjoram
☐ Few drops olive oil   ☐ Salt and pepper

---

1. Roll the dough out into a round on a lightly floured surface.

2. Spread the tomato sauce over the dough.

3. Arrange the 3 different pepper slices evenly over the tomato sauce.

4. Place slices of Mozzarella over the peppers. Season with salt, pepper and the marjoram.

5. Sprinkle over a little olive oil and cook in a very hot oven for approximately 10 to 15 minutes.

TIME   Preparation takes about 20 minutes and cooking takes approximately 10 to 15 minutes.

SERVING IDEA   The Mozzarella can be cut into small cubes and scattered over the pizza at Step 4. This is particularly appropriate if the Mozzarella is a little dry.

FREEZER IDEA   This type of pizza can only be frozen once it has been cooked and is completely cold. Reheat in a microwave for a few minutes with a little olive oil.

☐

OPPOSITE

PEPPER PIZZA

SERVES 4

SEAFOOD PIZZA

*A seafood special with cockles and mussels
which have been opened in white wine.
A sumptuous pizza for special occasions.*

Step 5

Step 5

Step 6

☐ 1 quantity bread dough (see Wild Mushroom Pizza recipe)
☐ 1 quantity tomato sauce (see Mozzarella Pizza recipe)
☐ 8oz cockles   ☐ 1lb mussels
☐ 1 large onion, finely sliced   ☐ 2 cloves garlic, chopped
☐ 4 tbsps Parmesan cheese, chopped
☐ ½ cup white wine   ☐ 1 tsp marjoram
☐ Salt and pepper

---

1. Wash, brush and rinse the cockles and mussels well. Place them in a large saucepan, pour over the white wine and place over a high heat, shaking the pan frequently until all the shells have opened. Set the pan aside to allow the contents to cool.

2. Once the cockles and mussels are cooled, remove them from their shells, discarding any that have not opened.

3. Roll out the dough into a large round on a floured surface.

4. Pour the tomato sauce into the center of the pizza, spreading it over the dough with the back of a tablespoon.

5. Place the sliced onion over the tomato sauce, then the mussels and the cockles.

6. Scatter over the garlic, and season with the marjoram, salt, pepper and Parmesan cheese.

7. Cook in a very hot oven for approximately 15 to 25 minutes, depending on the thickness of the dough. Serve immediately.

TIME   Preparation takes about 25 minutes and cooking takes approximately 40 minutes.

COOK'S TIP   Frozen cockles and mussels can be used, thus cutting down on preparation time.

VARIATION   Use lots of different types of seafood, such as shrimp, clams, crab – the pizza will be so much the better for the variety. If preferred, the dough can be formed into 4 individual pizzas, reducing cooking time to between 15 and 20 minutes.

☐

OPPOSITE

SEAFOOD PIZZA

—— SERVES 4 ——

GOAT CHEESE PIZZA

*Flavored with goat cheese and bacon,
this pizza is that little bit different.*

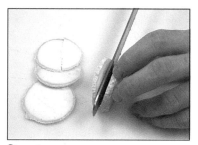

Step 4

☐ 1 quantity bread dough (see Wild Mushroom Pizza recipe)
☐ 1 quantity tomato sauce (see Mozzarella Pizza recipe)
☐ 1 onion, finely sliced   ☐ 2 goat cheeses
☐ 1 tbsp marjoram, chopped   ☐ 4 strips bacon
☐ Salt and pepper

1. Roll the dough out thinly on a floured surface.

2. Spread the tomato sauce over the dough and then sprinkle over the onion.

3. Cut the bacon into small pieces and scatter over the pizza.

4. Slice the goat cheese with a finely serrated knife and lay the slices over the pizza.

5. Season with salt and pepper, sprinkle over the marjoram and cook in a very hot oven for approximately 15 minutes. This pizza cooks quite quickly, as the dough is fairly thin.

TIME   Preparation takes about 20 minutes and cooking takes approximately 15 minutes.

SERVING IDEA   Hot pepper olive oil is particularly good with this pizza.

COOK'S TIP   Using a finely serrated knife when cutting the goat cheese helps prevent it from crumbling.

☐

OPPOSITE

GOAT CHEESE
PIZZA

—— SERVES 4 ——

INDIVIDUAL PIZZAS WITH EGG

*Small, individual pizzas, coated with tomato sauce,
onion, bacon and an egg. Make a meal of one of
these pizzas with a tossed salad.*

Step 3

Step 5

☐ 1 quantity bread dough (see Wild Mushroom Pizza recipe)
☐ 1 quantity tomato sauce (see Mozzarella Pizza recipe)
☐ 1 large onion, finely sliced   ☐ 4 eggs
☐ 4 strips bacon, cut into small pieces
☐ 4 tbsps grated Parmesan cheese   ☐ Salt and pepper

1. Form the dough into 4 equal balls. Roll each ball out on a floured surface into a thin round.

2. Pour about 5 tbsps of the tomato sauce over each round, spreading it evenly over the dough.

3. Sprinkle the onion and then the bacon evenly over the 4 pizzas.

4. Season with salt and pepper.

5. Break one egg over each pizza and sprinkle over the grated Parmesan.

6. Cook in a very hot oven for 10 to 15 minutes. Serve immediately.

TIME   Preparation takes about 20 minutes and cooking takes approximately 15 minutes, depending on the thickness of the dough.

COOK'S TIP   If you prefer your egg yolks to remain runny, break the eggs onto the pizzas halfway through the cooking time.

WATCHPOINT   Do not spread the egg white out onto the pizza; the egg will spread over the pizza by itself during cooking.

☐

OPPOSITE

INDIVIDUAL PIZZAS
WITH EGG

— SERVES 4 —

OCTOPUS AND SQUID SALAD

A delicious fish salad of octopus and squid coated in a tasty sauce of lemon juice, olive oil, herbs and garlic.

Step 1

Step 1

□ 1 large lettuce   □ ¾ lb squid   □ ¾ lb octopus
□ 2 tbsps lemon juice   □ 2 tbsps olive oil
□ Salt and pepper   □ ½ tsp chopped marjoram
□ 1 tsp chopped parsley   □ 1 clove garlic, chopped

1. Empty and wash the squid and the octopus.

2. Cook them in boiling water for approximately 30 minutes, or until cooked through and reasonably tender.

3. Rinse under cold water and set aside to drain. Once well drained, cut them into thin rounds and then into small dice.

4. Mix together the lemon juice, olive oil, salt, pepper, marjoram, garlic and the parsley.

5. Mix the squid and octopus into the sauce and leave to marinate for a few hours.

6. Wash the lettuce, chop or shred the leaves and place on 4 individual plates.

7. Serve the prepared octopus and squid on the prepared lettuce with the marinade poured over.

TIME   Preparation takes about 40 minutes and cooking takes approximately 30 minutes.

COOK'S TIP   Prepare this dish the day before serving so that the flavors have a chance to develop.

WATCHPOINT   If the octopus is very large, beat it lightly with a rolling pin before cooking, as one would to tenderize steak; this will help it to cook better.

□

OPPOSITE

OCTOPUS AND
SQUID SALAD

— SERVES 4 —

STUFFED ZUCCHINI FLOWERS

*A rich and creamy fish stuffing is used to fill
zucchini flowers, which are then steamed
and served in a herb and cream sauce.*

Step 2

Step 3

Step 4

☐ 12 zucchini flowers, delicately washed and dried
☐ 1 cup whitefish flesh ☐ 1 egg
☐ 1½ cups light cream ☐ 1 tbsp heavy cream
☐ 3 tbsps chopped chives ☐ Salt and pepper

1. Place the fish, 1 tbsp chopped chives, the egg and 1 tbsp of light cream in a food processor. Process until smooth.

2. Push the fish mixture through a fine sieve and season with salt and pepper. Place in the refrigerator for 30 minutes.

3. Beat the heavy cream into the fish stuffing and place the stuffing in a pastry bag fitted with a plain tube.

4. Gently ease open the leaves of the zucchini flowers and fill the center with the stuffing.

5. Form the outer leaves back into shape and set the flowers to cook in a steamer for approximately 12 minutes.

6. Heat the remaining light cream with the remaining chives and serve the zucchini flowers with the sauce poured over.

TIME   Preparation takes about 30 minutes and cooking takes approximately 20 minutes. Chiling time for the stuffing is 30 minutes.

VARIATION   Add a little grated Mozzarella or Parmesan cheese to the stuffing.

WATCHPOINT   Heat the cream at Step 6 over a very gentle heat; do not allow it to boil.

☐

OPPOSITE

STUFFED
ZUCCHINI
FLOWERS

—— SERVES 4 ——

VEGETABLE RISOTTO

*Risotto is a highly adaptable and ever popular
rice dish; try this vegetable version as a
change from the everyday chicken variety.*

Step 1

Step 1

☐ 2 large leaves chard   ☐ ½ onion, finely chopped
☐ 1 carrot, diced   ☐ 1¾ cups rice
☐ ¾ cup frozen peas   ☐ 1 thick slice ham, diced
☐ 1 stick celery, diced   ☐ ¼ cup butter   ☐ Salt and pepper

1. Cut the green leaf part of the chard into very thin strips and
then cut the white stalk into small dice.

2. Heat the butter in a large frying pan and fry the onion, carrot,
celery and the green and white parts of the chard for 2 minutes.

3. Add the rice, peas and ham to the frying pan, stir well and cook
until the rice is transparent.

4. Transfer to an ovenproof dish and pour over water equivalent
to 1½ times the volume of the rice. Season with salt and pepper
and stir well.

5. Cover the dish and cook in a hot oven, 400°F, for between
18 and 20 minutes. Serve hot.

TIME   Preparation takes about 15 minutes and cooking takes
approximately 30 minutes.

VARIATION   The chard can be replaced with the same
quantity of spinach.

COOK'S TIP   A little garlic or bacon added to the frying pan at
Step 2 will improve the flavor still further.

☐

OPPOSITE

VEGETABLE
RISOTTO

---- SERVES 4 ----

STUFFED ZUCCHINI

*Round, plump zucchini filled with
a meaty beef and herb stuffing
make a very filling dish.*

Step 3

Step 3

Step 4

☐ 12 small, round zucchini, washed
☐ 1 cup (firmly packed) ground beef ☐ ½ onion, finely chopped
☐ 1 tbsp chopped tarragon ☐ Salt and pepper
☐ 2 tbsps olive oil ☐ 1 egg
☐ 1 clove garlic, chopped

1. Cut off the ends of the zucchini and hollow out the centers with a small spoon.

2. Bring a saucepan of water to the boil and plunge in the zucchini for 30 seconds. Drain upside down and set aside until needed.

3. Mix together the beef, onion, tarragon, salt and pepper. Stir well to combine the ingredients thoroughly.

4. Finally add the egg, mixing well to bind the stuffing together.

5. Season the hollowed out centers of the zucchini with salt and pepper and spoon in the stuffing.

6. Place the zucchini in an ovenproof dish and sprinkle over the olive oil.

7. Place a little garlic on each zucchini and then cook in a hot oven for approximately 30 minutes.

TIME   Preparation takes about 30 minutes and cooking takes approximately 30 minutes.

VARIATION   Add 1 tbsp Cognac to the stuffing for a richer flavor.

COOK'S TIP   If the zucchini have absorbed a lot of water during Step 2, pat them dry with paper towels after draining.

☐

OPPOSITE

STUFFED
ZUCCHINI

—————— SERVES 4 ——————

SICILIAN RATATOUILLE

*Cooked in a casserole, this warming blend of
Mediterranean vegetables makes for a
mouthwatering vegetable accompaniment.*

Step 2

☐ 1 eggplant, cut into small cubes
☐ 1 large onion, sliced
☐ 3 large tomatoes, peeled, seeded and roughly chopped
☐ ½ stick celery, cut into small pieces
☐ 10 green olives, stoned   ☐ 1 tsp capers
☐ 2 tbsps olive oil   ☐ 1 tsp chopped garlic
☐ 1 tsp chopped parsley   ☐ Salt and pepper
☐ Oil for deep frying

1. Fry the eggplant in moderately hot oil, taking care that they do not turn brown. Remove with a slotted spoon and drain on kitchen paper.

2. Cut the stoned olives into thin rounds.

3. Heat the olive oil in a casserole and cook the celery, onion, olives, capers, garlic and parsley together for 1 minute.

4. Stir in the chopped tomato and fried eggplant and season with salt and pepper.

5. Cook on a gentle heat for approximately 30 minutes. Stir gently, from time to time, to prevent sticking.

TIME   Preparation takes about 15 minutes, frying takes approximately 4 minutes and cooking time is at least 30 minutes.

VARIATION   Replace the parsley with the same quantity of basil.

WATCHPOINT   When frying the eggplant, watch them carefully as they cook very quickly and will turn brown if not removed as soon as they turn a golden color.

☐

OPPOSITE

SICILIAN
RATATOUILLE

—— SERVES 4 ——

EGGPLANT SCAPECE

*Fried eggplant slices are coated with a tasty paste of
anchovy, garlic and vinegar, left to marinate for a
short time and served at room temperature.*

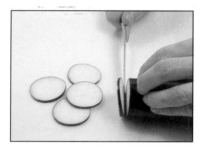

□ 2 large, unblemished eggplants, cut into rounds
□ 4 anchovy fillets, boned   □ 1 clove garlic
□ 1 tbsp parsley   □ ½ cup Xeres or wine vinegar
□ ½ tsp hot pepper paste   □ Salt and pepper
□ Oil for deep frying

Step 1

Step 1

1. Heat the oil until moderately hot, and gently fry the eggplant slices. Do not allow them to turn brown. Set aside on paper towels to drain.

2. In a mortar and pestle, crush together the anchovies, parsley, hot pepper paste and garlic. Season with salt and a little pepper.

3. Stir the vinegar into the above mixture.

4. Spread the eggplant slices out onto a large serving plate and pour over the anchovy sauce.

5. Marinate for 1½ hours and serve at room temperature.

TIME   Preparation takes about 30 minutes and marinating time is 1½ hours.

VARIATION   One could use zucchini with the eggplant and add a little finely chopped onion to the sauce. If hot pepper paste is not available, mix a few drops Tabasco with a little tomato paste as an alternative.

COOK'S TIP   If prepared the day before serving, the flavor will be stronger. The dish should be marinated in the refrigerator and removed 2 hours before serving.

□

OPPOSITE

EGGPLANT
SCAPECE

SERVES 4

RED SNAPPER SALAD

*Complemented by a marvelous fish
sauce, red snapper fillets are served with
diced tomatoes and a green salad.*

Step 2

Step 2

Step 3

- ☐ 12 small red snapper   ☐ 1 carrot, sliced   ☐ 1 onion, sliced
- ☐ ¼ cup white wine   ☐ 4 small servings mixed green salad
- ☐ 1 tomato, seeded and cut into small cubes
- ☐ ½ tbsp wine vinegar   ☐ 4 tbsps olive oil
- ☐ 2 tbsp butter   ☐ Small bunch chives   ☐ Salt and pepper

1. Gut and fillet the fish. Keep the heads and the bones. Set the fillets aside in a cool place until needed.

2. Melt the butter in a frying pan and fry the carrot and onion for 1 minute, then stir in the heads and bones from the fish. Cook for 1 minute, stirring continuously.

3. Deglaze the pan with the white wine, stir well and the pour in 1 cup water. Cook for 15 minutes.

4. Strain this sauce through a very fine sieve and reduce over a high heat to about ¼ cup.

5. Season the fillets with salt and pepper.

6. Heat 2 tbsps olive oil in a frying pan and quickly fry the fillets on both sides for a few minutes. Drain the fillets on paper towels.

7. Mix together the fish sauce, vinegar and the remaining olive oil. Taste and adjust seasoning as necessary.

8. Place a little mixed green salad on 4 plates and sprinkle over the tomato. Finely chop almost all of the chives and mix them into the sauce.

9. Place the warm fish fillets on the salad and pour over a little of the sauce. Decorate the plates with sprigs of chives.

TIME   Preparation takes about 30 minutes and cooking takes approximately 30 minutes.

COOK'S TIP   When frying the fillets, fry them skin-side down first so that they do not shrink.

VARIATION   A small rock crab may be added to the fish stock sauce to give it a stronger flavor.

☐

OPPOSITE

RED SNAPPER
SALAD

— SERVES 4 —

GOAT CHEESE SALAD WITH TARRAGON

*Goat cheese slices served on bread rounds
and accompanied by a
tarragon-flavored salad.*

Step 1

Step 2

Step 3

☐ 12 small slices white bread
☐ 4 small goat cheeses (not too fresh)
☐ 4 small servings of mixed green salad, washed and dried
☐ 1 tbsp chopped fresh tarragon
☐ 1 tbsp tarragon vinegar   ☐ 2 tbsps olive oil
☐ Salt and pepper

1. Using a pastry cutter, cut the sliced bread into 12 rounds.

2. Cut each cheese horizontally into 3 rounds and place on the prepared bread rounds.

3. Sprinkle the chopped tarragon over the cheese rounds.

4. To prepare the dressing, mix together the tarragon vinegar, olive oil, salt and pepper. Stir or shake well and pour over the prepared mixed green salad.

5. Place the cheese and bread rounds into a moderately hot oven and cook until the cheese melts slightly and the top is golden.

6. Remove from the oven and set the cheese and toast rounds onto the tossed salad.

TIME   Preparation takes about 25 minutes and cooking takes approximately 5 minutes.

VARIATION   Red wine vinegar can be substituted for the tarragon vinegar if preferred.

COOK'S TIP   Cut the bread to the same size as the cheese rounds; this way the cheese will completely cover the bread and the bread will not burn in the oven.

☐

OPPOSITE

GOAT CHEESE
SALAD WITH
TARRAGON

—— SERVES 4 ——

CHICKEN LIVER SALAD

*Delicately flavored with shallot and parsley, this quick
and easy salad is ideal for the busy hostess.*

Step 3

Step 5

☐ 12 chicken livers   ☐ 1 shallot, finely chopped
☐ 3 tbsps Xeres or wine vinegar
☐ 2 cloves garlic, finely chopped
☐ 1 tbsp parsley   ☐ 4 slices white bread
☐ 1 tomato, cut into small dice   ☐ ¼ cup butter
☐ ⅓ cup olive oil
☐ 4 small servings of shredded mixed green salad

1. Cut the slices of bread into small, even-sized cubes.

2. Heat 2 tbsps olive oil in a frying pan and quickly fry the bread cubes over a high heat. Fry until lightly golden and then tip out onto paper towels to drain.

3. Melt the butter in the same pan and gently fry the chicken livers.

4. Once the livers are cooked through (cut one to check that the centers are not too pink), add the shallot, garlic and parsley.

5. Fry for a few minutes and then deglaze the pan with 2 tbsps vinegar.

6. Place the prepared green salad onto 4 plates and tip the livers evenly over the 4 plates.

7. Mix together the remaining vinegar, olive oil and a little salt and pepper. Shake or stir well to form a vinaigrette dressing.

8. Sprinkle the diced tomato and the croutons over the chicken livers and pour over a little dressing. The dish can be served immediately, or you may prefer to serve when the livers are cold.

TIME   Preparation takes approximately 40 minutes and cooking takes about 5 minutes.

COOK'S TIP   The chicken livers may be served slightly underdone if preferred.

WATCHPOINT   It is important to let the croutons drain on kitchen paper as they tend to absorb a lot of oil during frying.

☐

OPPOSITE

CHICKEN LIVER
SALAD

---- SERVES 4 ----

STUFFED WHITE ONIONS

*Mild white Italian onions stuffed with veal
and sprinkled with Parmesan cheese;
a delicious recipe that begs to be tried.*

Step 1

Step 2

Step 5

☐ 12 white Italian onions, peeled ☐ 8oz veal
☐ 1 tbsp chopped parsley ☐ 1 tsp Madeira
☐ 1 tbsp olive oil ☐ 2 tbsps grated Parmesan cheese
☐ Salt and pepper

1. Cook the peeled onions in lightly salted, boiling water for 10 minutes. Drain well.

2. Hollow out the center of each onion, reserving the scooped out onion flesh.

3. Finely chop the reserved onion flesh.

4. Grind the meat in a food processor and then stir in the chopped onion, parsley, Madeira and 1 tsp of olive oil. Season with salt and pepper.

5. Fill each hollowed-out onion with the veal mixture.

6. Grease an ovenproof dish with the remaining olive oil and place the onions in the dish.

7. Cook in a hot oven for 15 minutes, then sprinkle the grated Parmesan cheese over each stuffed onion.

TIME   Preparation takes about 15 minutes and cooking takes approximately 30 minutes.

VARIATION   Replace the veal with turkey, beef or pork.

WATCHPOINT   Ensure that you leave sufficient onion to form a shell when hollowing out the center.

☐

OPPOSITE

STUFFED WHITE
ONIONS

—— SERVES 4 ——

POTATO CAKES

*Served hot and crispy,
these potato cakes
go well with meat dishes.*

Step 1

Step 1

Step 1

☐ 4 large potatoes, peeled and finely grated
☐ 1 tbsp chopped parsley
☐ 1 tbsp finely grated onion ☐ 4 tbsps olive oil
☐ Salt and pepper

1. Mix together the potato, parsley and onion. Season with plenty of salt and pepper.

2. Heat 1 tbsp olive oil in a non-stick frying pan.

3. Place one quarter of the potato mixture in the frying pan and flatten out with the back of a spoon into a largish round.

4. Cook over a gentle heat until crisp and golden on one side, then turn and cook the other side.

5. Repeat with the remaining mixture until you have 4 potato cakes.

6. Keep the potato cakes warm in a low oven until required.

TIME   Preparation takes about 5 minutes and cooking takes approximately 20 minutes for all 4 cakes.

WATCHPOINT   These potato cakes should be thin and crispy when served. Make sure that you spread them thinly in the frying pan.

VARIATION   Try different mixes of herbs instead of the parsley.

☐

OPPOSITE

POTATO CAKES

ROMAN-STYLE ARTICHOKES

*Artichoke hearts coated in a
basil-flavoured tomato sauce
and sprinkled with Parmesan cheese.*

Step 2

Step 2

Step 3

□ 16 small artichokes □ Juice of 2 lemons
□ 4 large tomatoes, peeled, seeded and roughly chopped
□ 1 tbsp chopped chives □ 2 tbsps olive oil
□ 5 fresh basil leaves, chopped □ Salt and pepper
□ 4 tbsps grated Parmesan cheese

1. Fill a bowl with water and add the lemon juice.

2. Cut the hard stalk ends off of the artichokes and, using a small, sharp knife, cut off all the leaves, leaving the hearts whole.

3. Place the artichoke hearts in the bowl of lemon water as soon as the leaves are removed, to prevent discoloration.

4. Cook the artichoke hearts in salted, boiling water, testing them for doneness with the point of a sharp knife.

5. Mix together the chives, tomato, 1 tbsp olive oil, basil and plenty of salt and pepper.

6. Remove the choke from each artichoke heart. Grease an ovenproof dish with the remaining oil and place the hearts in the dish.

7. Spoon the tomato sauce onto each heart, sprinkle over the Parmesan cheese and crisp up in a hot oven. Serve hot.

TIME   Preparation takes about 20 minutes and cooking takes approximately 40 minutes.

VARIATION   Use 4 large artichokes instead of small ones.

COOK'S TIP   Use a very sharp knife to cut off the leaves as they are very hard.

□

OPPOSITE

ROMAN-STYLE
ARTICHOKES

SERVES 4

ROMANY EGGPLANT

Enlivened by a tangy tomato sauce, bacon and ham, this tasty eggplant dish is surprisingly easy to prepare.

Step 1

Step 3

Step 4

☐ 2 large eggplants ☐ 1 thick strip bacon
☐ 1 slice ham ☐ 1 slice Parma ham
☐ 2 tbsps olive oil ☐ 2 tbsps butter
☐ 1 onion, chopped ☐ ½ tsp chopped rosemary
☐ 1 shallot, chopped ☐ 3 tbsps crushed tomato pulp
☐ ¼ cup white wine ☐ Salt and pepper

1. Cut the eggplants into slices.

2. Bring to the boil a large saucepan of lightly salted water.

3. Plunge the slices of eggplant into the boiling water and cook for 2 minutes.

4. Remove the eggplant slices from the water, drain and then set on paper towels to absorb any excess water.

5. Cut the bacon, ham and Parma ham into thin strips.

6. Heat the oil and the butter together in a frying pan and gently fry the onion, shallot, rosemary, the hams and the bacon together for a few minutes.

7. Stir in the tomato pulp and the white wine. Season with salt and pepper.

8. Spread the well-drained eggplant slices over the tomato sauce and cook, covered, for 5 minutes.

9. Remove the cover and continue cooking until the sauce has thickened and the juices have almost evaporated. Serve either hot or cold.

TIME   Preparation takes about 20 minutes and cooking takes approximately 1 hour and 10 minutes.

VARIATION   Once the dish is cooked, transfer to an ovenproof dish, cover with either Parmesan or Mozzarella cheese and cook in a hot oven until crisp and brown on the top.

WATCHPOINT   Do not cut the eggplant too thinly, otherwise they will break up during the final cooking stage.

☐

OPPOSITE

ROMANY
EGGPLANT

—— SERVES 4 ——

TOMATO SALAD

*With the added piquancy of capers
and a delicious sauce, this
is a tomato salad with a difference.*

Step 1

Step 2

Step 3

☐ 4 large tomatoes, each cut into 6 segments
☐ 1 onion, finely chopped   ☐ 1 tsp pickled capers
☐ 20 anchovy fillets in oil   ☐ Salt and pepper
☐ 1 tsp wine vinegar   ☐ 3 tbsps olive oil
☐ 4 servings mixed green salad, washed, dried and shredded

1.   Place the capers and 5 anchovy fillets in a mortar and pound into a smooth paste.

2.   Work the salt, pepper and vinegar into the above and transfer to a large bowl.

3.   To make the sauce, stir the olive oil, little by little, into the above paste.

4.   Arrange the prepared green salad evenly on 4 small plates and add the tomato.

5.   Spoon over the sauce, decorate with the reserved anchovies and sprinkle over the chopped onion.

TIME   Preparation takes approximately 30 minutes.

VARIATION   Finely slice fresh basil leaves and add them to the sauce before spooning it over the salad.

WATCHPOINT   Do not add too much salt at Step 2, as the anchovies are rather salty.

☐

OPPOSITE

TOMATO SALAD

— SERVES 4 —

FRIED ZUCCHINI AND ZUCCHINI FLOWERS

Flavored with anchovies and garlic,
the batter lends this attractive dish
an unusual flavor

Step 3

Step 3

Step 4

□ ½ clove garlic   □ 6 anchovy fillets
□ ⅔ cup warm water   □ 1¼ cups flour, sifted
□ 2 tbsps olive oil   □ Salt and pepper
□ Whites of 2 eggs
□ 20 small zucchini with their flowers intact, carefully washed
and patted dry with paper towels
□ Oil for deep frying

1. Pound the garlic and anchovies together in a mortar until quite smooth.

2. Mix this smooth paste into the warm water.

3. Place the flour in a large mixing bowl and whisk in the water and then the olive oil. Season with salt and pepper and set aside.

4. Stiffly beat the egg whites until they hold their form, and fold gently into the above batter.

5. Heat the oil to approximately 345°F.

6. Dip the zucchini and their flowers, one by one, into the batter and then fry them quickly in the oil.

7. Remove when crisp and golden, and set aside to drain on kitchen paper.

TIME   Preparation takes about 25 minutes and cooking takes approximately 20 minutes.

SERVING IDEA   Serve with quartered lemon and a mixed salad.

WATCHPOINT   Take particular care when folding the beaten egg white into the batter so as not to lose the bulk.

□

OPPOSITE

FRIED ZUCCHINI
AND ZUCCHINI
FLOWERS

—— SERVES 4 ——

JUMBO SHRIMP SALAD

*A mouthwatering sauce complements the
sautéed shrimp in this delicious salad.*

Step 1

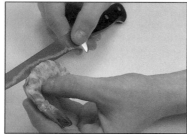

Step 1

Step 1

☐ 20 fresh jumbo shrimp ☐ 2 tbsps olive oil
☐ 1 carrot, finely sliced ☐ 1 tbsp crushed tomato pulp
☐ ½ onion, finely sliced ☐ ½ bay leaf ☐ 1 tsp Cognac
☐ 1 tbsp heavy cream ☐ ¼ cup butter
☐ 1 tsp Xeres or wine vinegar
☐ 4 small servings fancy leaf lettuce ☐ Salt and pepper

1. Peel and devein the shrimp, discarding the heads, but retaining the peelings for the sauce.

2. To make the sauce, heat 1 tbsp oil and fry the carrot, onion, tomato pulp, the peelings from the shrimp and the ½ bay leaf. Fry for 2 minutes and then tip off the excess fat.

3. Deglaze the pan with the Cognac and pour water over to cover the ingredients.

4. Continue cooking, reducing the liquid until it is quite thick. Stir in the cream and bring the sauce to the boil.

5. Strain through a very fine sieve, pressing the peelings to extract the juice.

6. Melt the butter in a frying pan and sauté the shrimp for 2 minutes.

7. Stir the vinegar into the shrimp sauce. Season with salt and pepper and then whisk in the remaining olive oil.

8. Serve the shrimp on a bed of washed, dried and chopped lettuce, with the sauce spooned over.

TIME   Preparation takes about 45 minutes and cooking takes approximately 30 minutes.

SERVING IDEA   Add diced tomato and a little finely diced green pepper to the salad.

WATCHPOINT   When reducing the shrimp sauce, reduce to about ⅓ cup then add the vinegar, a little at a time, as well as the oil, and season to taste.

☐

OPPOSITE

JUMBO SHRIMP
SALAD

SAUTEED BROCCOLI WITH GARLIC

*Slightly crisp broccoli tips
are sautéed in butter
and lots of garlic.*

Step 1

Step 1

Step 2

□ 2lbs broccoli, washed
□ 2 cloves garlic, chopped   □ ¼ cup butter
□ 2 tsps chopped parsley   □ Salt and pepper

1. Cut the broccoli into flowerets and trim off the stalks.

2. Cook all the parts of the broccoli in salted, boiling water for 5 minutes.

3. Rinse in cold water to freshen and set aside to drain.

4. Melt the butter in a frying pan, stir in the garlic and parsley and then add the broccoli flowerets. Fry for a few minutes.

5. Season with plenty of salt and pepper and serve hot.

TIME   Preparation takes about 10 minutes and cooking takes approximately 20 minutes.

WATCHPOINT   Do not overcook the broccoli in the salted, boiling water, otherwise they will be reduced to a pulp in the frying pan.

COOK'S TIP   When the stalks are cooked through (this takes slightly longer than for the tips), drain them well and then blend with a hand mixer into a smooth purée. Serve this under the sautéed broccoli.

□

OPPOSITE

SAUTEED
BROCCOLI WITH
GARLIC

SICILIAN CANNELLONI

Cannelloni stuffed with meat, covered with slices of Mozzarella and cooked in a chicken stock until crisp and golden on top.

Step 2

Step 2

☐ 16 cannelloni   ☐ 4 mushrooms, rinsed and chopped
☐ ¾ lb braising beef, ground   ☐ 1 shallot, chopped
☐ 2 slices ham, chopped   ☐ 10 thin slices Mozzarella cheese
☐ ¼ cup butter   ☐ ½ cup chicken stock
☐ Butter for greasing   ☐ Salt and pepper

1. Pre-cook the cannelloni in salted, boiling water for 1 minute. Set aside to drain.

2. Melt the butter in a saucepan or casserole and cook the shallot, mushrooms, ham and beef for approximately 10 minutes. Season with salt and pepper and set aside to cool.

3. When the stuffing is cool, fill the cannelloni and place in a lightly-greased, ovenproof dish.

4. Place the slices of Mozzarella over the cannelloni and then pour over the chicken stock.

5. Cook in a hot oven for approximately 15 to 25 minutes – the dish should be heated through and the top should be crisp and golden. Serve piping hot.

TIME   Preparation takes about 15 minutes, cooling takes about 15 minutes and cooking time is up to 25 minutes.

VARIATION   Use different sorts of wild mushrooms, if available, in this cannelloni recipe.

COOK'S TIP   Once the cannelloni are cooked, spread them out onto a damp tea towel to prevent them from sticking together.

☐

OPPOSITE

SICILIAN
CANNELLONI

TAGLIATELLE WITH SAUTEED VEGETABLES

Fresh tagliatelle served with sautéed vegetables.

Step 2

Step 3

Step 3

PASTA DOUGH

☐ 3 cups all-purpose flour, sifted   ☐ 2 eggs, beaten
☐ Pinch salt

☐ 2 zucchini thickly peeled (keep the peel and discard the rest)
☐ 1 red pepper, seeded and cut into thin strips
☐ ¼ cup butter   ☐ 2 tbsps olive oil   ☐ Salt and pepper

1. Make the dough by mixing together the flour, eggs and a good pinch of salt. Work the dough with your fingertips and form into a ball. Set aside to rest in the refrigerator for 30 minutes.

2. Pass the dough through the rollers of a pasta machine, flouring the dough well to prevent sticking. Alternatively, roll out the dough with a rolling pin.

3. Pass the strips through the pasta machine fitted with a tagliatelle cutter. Spread the tagliatelle out on a tea towel and leave to dry for 30 minutes. If a pasta machine is not being used, cut the rolled dough into tagliatelle strips with a knife.

4. Heat the olive oil in a frying pan and sauté the pepper for 2 minutes, stirring frequently. Add strips of the zucchini peel and continue cooking for 45 seconds. Pour off the excess fat and season with salt and pepper. Keep warm.

5. Cook the tagliatelle in salted, boiling water for a few minutes, rinse under hot water and set to drain.

6. Set the frying pan containing the vegetables over the heat, stir in the butter and then stir in the tagliatelle. Heat the tagliatelle through thoroughly and serve immediately.

TIME   Preparation takes about 50 minutes and cooking takes approximately 20 minutes.

VARIATION   Use other vegetables such as cucumber and carrot in this recipe. Cut the vegetables into very thin strips and proceed as above.

WATCHPOINT   If you have made your own tagliatelle, watch the cooking really closely, as fresh, home-made pasta cooks much more quickly than the dried variety.

☐

OPPOSITE

TAGLIATELLE WITH SAUTEÈD VEGETABLES

MEAT RAVIOLI WITH RED PEPPER SAUCE

*Red-tinged, pepper-flavored pasta dough is rolled thinly,
cut into squares, filled with a delicious meat stuffing
and served with a creamy red pepper sauce.*

Step 2

Step 2

Step 3

☐ 2 red peppers, seeded   ☐ 2 cups all-purpose flour, sifted
☐ 2 eggs   ☐ 1 cup ground beef
☐ 1 tbsp finely chopped parsley
☐ ½ onion, chopped   ☐ ½ cup light cream
☐ ⅓ cup butter   ☐ Salt and pepper

1. Place the red peppers in a food processor and blend until liquid. Place in a small bowl and set aside, giving time for the pulp to rise to the surface. This takes approximately 30 minutes.

2. To make the dough, place the sifted flour in a bowl with a pinch of salt. Add 1 egg and 3 tbsps of the pulp (not the juice).

3. Mix together really well and form into a ball. Set the dough aside for 30 minutes.

4. Mix together the meat, parsley and onion and season with salt and pepper.

5. Roll the dough out very thinly, using a pasta machine if available, and cut into small squares. Place a little stuffing on half of the cut squares. Beat the remaining egg and brush the edges of the squares with the egg. Cover with another square of dough and seal the edges by pinching together with your fingers.

6. Bring a large saucepan of salted water to the boil and cook the ravioli for approximately 3 minutes – longer if you prefer your pasta well cooked.

7. While the ravioli are cooking, prepare the sauce by heating the cream with ½ cup of the red pepper pulp. Bring to the boil and then whisk in the butter.

8. Drain the ravioli and then pat them dry with a tea towel. Serve with the hot cream sauce.

TIME   Preparation takes about 50 minutes, resting time 30 minutes and cooking time approximately 15 minutes.

VARIATION   Add a little wine vinegar (1 tsp) and a few drops of Tabasco to the sauce to give it a slightly peppery taste.

WATCHPOINT   When rolling out the dough, flour it well so that it does not stick to the rolling pin or pasta machine rollers.

☐

OPPOSITE

MEAT RAVIOLI
WITH RED PEPPER
SAUCE

---- SERVES 4 ----

SPAGHETTI CARBONARA

*Spaghetti served in a rich sauce of
cream, egg yolks, bacon and capers.*

Step 3

Step 4

☐ 1lb spaghetti   ☐ 2 strips bacon, cut into small pieces
☐ 1 tbsp capers   ☐ ¾ cup light cream
☐ ¼ cup milk   ☐ 4 egg yolks   ☐ Salt and pepper

1. Cook the spaghetti in salted, boiling water. When cooked, drain, rinse in hot water and set aside to drain thoroughly.

2. Heat the milk and the cream in a saucepan. Season with salt and pepper.

3. Add the bacon and the capers and cook for 1 minute.

4. Add the drained spaghetti and cook until heated through completely.

5. Beat the egg yolks in a small bowl and then add them to the hot spaghetti. Remove the saucepan from the heat, stirring continuously with a wooden spoon, and serve.

TIME   Preparation takes about 5 minutes and cooking takes approximately 30 minutes.

SERVING IDEA   Sprinkle over a little grated Parmesan cheese just before serving.

WATCHPOINT   The spaghetti must be hot when the beaten egg yolk is added, so that the egg cooks in the residual heat.

☐

OPPOSITE

SPAGHETTI
CARBONARA

SALMON AND FENNEL LASAGNE

Thin strips of pasta are pre-cooked and then layered with salmon and bechamel sauce. Fish stock is poured over and the dish is then topped with cheese and cooked in the oven. Absolutely mouthwatering!

Step 3

Step 5

Step 5

- ☐ 3 ½ cups all-purpose flour, sifted   ☐ 3 eggs, beaten
- ☐ 1 cup fairly runny bechamel sauce
- ☐ 1⅓ lbs salmon (in one long strip if possible)
- ☐ 1 tsp fennel seeds   ☐ 4 tbsps grated cheese
- ☐ 1 cup fish stock   ☐ 2 tbsps butter
- ☐ Salt and pepper

1. Make the dough by mixing together the flour, a good pinch of salt and the 3 eggs. Set the dough aside to rest for 30 minutes and then roll out very thinly into long strips.

2. Part-cook the pasta in salted, boiling water for 1 minute. Drain and then lay out on damp tea towels, without overlapping the strips.

3. Cut the salmon into thin slices – a very sharp knife with a finely serrated blade is best for this delicate job. Remove all the bones.

4. Butter an ovenproof dish and place strips of pasta into the base.

5. Now build up layers of white sauce, a few fennel seeds, the salmon, salt, pepper and then another layer of pasta. Continue layering these ingredients until they are all used up, finishing with a layer of pasta.

6. Pour over the fish stock and then sprinkle over the cheese. Cook in a hot oven until the fish stock has been almost completely absorbed. Serve hot.

TIME   Preparation takes about 40 minutes and cooking takes approximately 35 minutes.

SERVING IDEA   This lasagne can be served with a cream sauce made by gently heating a little cream with 1 tsp fennel seeds.

COOK'S TIP   This lasagne should be slightly crisp and golden on top. If necessary, place the dish under a hot broiler for 1 minute.

☐

OPPOSITE

SALMON AND
FENNEL LASAGNE

—— SERVES 4 ——

FRESH PASTA WITH BOLOGNESE SAUCE

A rich, meaty sauce, cooked with white wine, carrots, onion and tomatoes.

Step 1

Step 3

☐ 2 ½ cups fresh pasta shells
☐ 1 carrot, cut into very small dice
☐ 1 onion, cut into small dice   ☐ 3 cups ground beef
☐ ½ cup white wine
☐ 3 tomatoes, peeled, seeded and chopped
☐ 1 bay leaf   ☐ 2 tbsps olive oil
☐ ¼ cup butter   ☐ ½ cup water   ☐ Salt and pepper

1. Heat the olive oil in a casserole and fry the carrot and onion until nicely browned.

2. Pour in the white wine and cook until the wine has completely evaporated.

3. Add the ground beef to the casserole and cook for 2 minutes, stirring well.

4. Into the casserole, pour ½ cup water and add the tomatoes and the bay leaf. Season with salt and pepper, stir well and cook over a gentle heat for a further 30 minutes.

5. When cooking time for the sauce is almost up, set the pasta shells to cook in a pan of salted, boiling water. Rinse the pasta and allow it to drain.

6. Melt the butter and stir it into the pasta shells, then pour over the sauce and serve immediately. Serve piping hot.

TIME   Preparation takes about 15 minutes and cooking takes approximately 50 minutes.

VARIATION   To make a slightly stronger flavored sauce, add a bouquet garni made up of thyme, parsley and garlic to the sauce at Step 4.

COOK'S TIP   Allow the wine to evaporate completely, so that the sauce is flavored by it and not affected by its acidity.

☐

OPPOSITE

FRESH PASTA WITH
BOLOGNESE SAUCE

COUNTRYSIDE SAUCE WITH FRESH PASTA

Made from ingredients that are common to most kitchens, this sauce is a delicious and quickly prepared stand-by for a last-minute supper.

Step 2

Step 2

□ ¾ lb fresh pasta   □ ¼ cup butter
□ 1 onion, sliced   □ 2 slices ham, cut into small pieces
□ 6 basil leaves, chopped   □ 2 tbsps crushed tomato
□ 2 tbsps grated Parmesan cheese   □ 1 tbsp olive oil
□ Salt and pepper

1. Cook the pasta in salted, boiling water to your liking. Rinse under hot water and set aside to drain.

2. Heat the olive oil in a frying pan and gently fry the onion, ham, basil and tomato for approximately 20 minutes. Season with salt and pepper.

3. Melt the butter in a saucepan and add the pasta, stirring well. Stir in the sauce and serve when the pasta is hot. Sprinkle over the grated Parmesan and serve.

TIME   Preparation takes 5 minutes and cooking takes approximately 20 minutes.

VARIATION   Try a little smoked ham in this dish.

COOK'S TIP   Most people prefer their pasta cooked "al dente", although you can boil the pasta a little longer if you prefer it somewhat softer.

□

OPPOSITE

COUNTRYSIDE
SAUCE WITH FRESH
PASTA

PASTA WITH BASIL AND WALNUT SAUCE

A tangy sauce made by pounding together walnuts, basil leaves and garlic.

Step 1

Step 4

Step 5

□ 1lb fresh pasta   □ 1 cup shelled walnuts
□ 15 basil leaves   □ ¼ clove garlic   □ 1 drop olive oil
□ ¼ cup butter   □ Salt and pepper

1. Pound together the walnuts, basil leaves and garlic in a mortar and pestle until a smooth paste is formed.

2. Cook the pasta in salted, boiling water for between 3 and 8 minutes, depending on how you like your pasta cooked. Rinse in hot water and set aside to drain.

3. Heat together in a saucepan the olive oil and butter.

4. Add the basil, walnut and garlic mixture to the saucepan, stirring well to combine all the ingredients.

5. Add the pasta to the pan, stir well and allow to heat through.

6. Check the seasoning and add salt and pepper as necessary. Serve immediately.

TIME   Preparation takes about 15 minutes and cooking takes approximately 15 minutes.

VARIATION   The walnuts could be replaced by almonds and/or hazelnuts if desired.

COOK'S TIP   If you have chosen large pasta for this recipe, it is better to reheat it prior to Step 5 by plunging it into boiling water and draining it rapidly before adding to the pan.

□

OPPOSITE

PASTA WITH BASIL
AND WALNUT
SAUCE

---- SERVES 4 ----

PASTA WITH COCKLES

Pasta served with cockles, butter and garlic.

Step 1

Step 2

□ 1lb cockles □ 1 shallot, chopped
□ ¾ lb fresh pasta □ 1 clove garlic, chopped
□ ¼ cup butter □ ½ tbsp chopped parsley
□ ½ cup white wine □ Salt and pepper

1. Place the cockles in a large saucepan, pour in the white wine, add the shallot and place over a high heat. Shake the saucepan frequently until the cockles open. Remove from the heat and set the pan aside until the cockles are cool enough to handle.

2. Remove the cockles from their shells.

3. Cook the pasta to your liking in salted, boiling water. Rinse in hot water and set aside to drain.

4. Melt the butter in a saucepan, add the garlic, chopped parsley, pasta and the cockles. Season with salt and pepper.

5. Keep on the heat, stirring well until the pasta is heated through. Serve immediately.

TIME   Preparation takes about 10 minutes and cooking takes approximately 20 minutes.

VARIATION   Other shellfish, such as whelks or clams, may be added to this dish.

COOK'S TIP   When the cockles are cooked and cooled, you can remove them from their shells, but keep them in the cooking juice until needed; this prevents them from drying out.

□

OPPOSITE

PASTA WITH
COCKLES

——— SERVES 4 ———

FRESH PASTA WITH GARLIC AND PARSLEY

Cooked fresh pasta served in butter,
olive oil, garlic and parsley sauce.

Step 2

Step 3

□ 1lb fresh pasta   □ 2 cloves garlic, finely chopped
□ 2 tbsps parsley, finely chopped   □ Few drops olive oil
□ ¼ cup butter   □ Salt and pepper

1. Cook the pasta to your liking in salted, boiling water. Rinse in hot water and set aside to drain.

2. Melt the butter in a frying pan, add the garlic and fry for 1 minute.

3. Add the drained pasta to the pan, stirring well to mix in the garlic. Cook for a few minutes.

4. Add a few drops of olive oil to the pan, remove from the heat and sprinkle over the parsley. Season with salt and pepper and serve.

TIME   Preparation takes about 5 minutes and cooking takes approximately 15 minutes.

COOK'S TIP   Mix together the butter, garlic and parsley. Keep in the refrigerator and use it for this dish when unexpected guests arrive.

VARIATION   If preferred, the butter may be substituted with olive oil.

□

OPPOSITE

FRESH PASTA WITH
GARLIC AND
PARSLEY

SPINACH TAGLIATELLE WITH CREAM SAUCE

*Fresh spinach pasta cooked in
boiling water and then served
with a creamy, chive-flavored sauce.*

Step 1

Step 2

Step 2

☐ 3 cups all-purpose flour, sifted ☐ 1 cup spinach, chopped
☐ 2 eggs ☐ 2 pinches salt ☐ 1 cup light cream
☐ 2 tbsps chopped chives ☐ Salt and pepper

1. Mix together the flour, 2 pinches of salt, eggs and spinach in a large bowl. Mix well and form the dough into a ball. Sprinkle the dough with flour and set aside in the refrigerator for 30 minutes.

2. Roll out the dough with a rolling pin or pass it through the rollers of the pasta machine and then cut it into tagliatelle strips.

3. Spread the strips out onto a floured surface; the strips should not touch one another. Allow to dry for a few minutes.

4. Bring to the boil a large pan of salted water, and cook the pasta 'al dente'. Rinse under hot water and set aside to drain.

5. Heat together the chives and cream, add the pasta to the saucepan, stir well and serve when the pasta is heated through. Season with a little salt and pepper if necessary.

TIME   Preparation takes about 45 minutes and cooking takes approximately 10 minutes.

COOK'S TIP   The use of a pasta machine is helpful in the making of fresh pasta. If you do not have one, use a rolling pin to roll the pasta dough out finely and then cut into the desired shape with a sharp knife. Always remember to flour the work surface and the utensils well.

WATCHPOINT   Ensure that the tagliatelle are well spread out when drying; this prevents them from sticking together during cooking.

☐

OPPOSITE

SPINACH
TAGLIATELLE WITH
CREAM SAUCE

—— SERVES 4 ——

HERB RAVIOLI WITH CHICKEN STOCK

Home-made ravioli dough is coated with fresh herbs and cooked in a chicken stock flavored with rosemary. This recipe is a soup and pasta dish combined.

Step 3

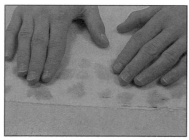

Step 4

Step 4

☐ 1¾ cups all-purpose flour, sifted   ☐ 1 egg, beaten
☐ 1 bunch chervil, washed and chopped
☐ 1 bunch parsley, washed and chopped
☐ 4 cups chicken stock   ☐ 1 tsp dried rosemary
☐ Salt and pepper

1. Make the dough by mixing together the flour, a good pinch of salt and the egg in a large bowl. Set aside to rest for 30 minutes.

2. Pass the dough through a pasta machine, flouring both sides of the dough as it goes through the rollers to prevent sticking. Cut the dough into long strips. Alternatively, roll the dough thinly with a rolling pin and cut into strips.

3. Spread out half of the strips onto your work surface and sprinkle over the chervil and parsley.

4. Place the remaining strips on top, press down well all along the strips with your fingers and then once again run the strips through the rollers of the pasta machine, or roll with a rolling pin.

5. Heat the stock and rosemary together in a saucepan until just boiling. Season with salt and pepper.

6. Cut the dough into the desired ravioli shapes.

7. Cook in the boiling stock for approximately 2 to 4 minutes. Serve very hot in shallow soup plates.

TIME   Preparation takes about 45 minutes and cooking takes about 10 minutes.

VARIATION   Herbs such as chives, basil, marjoram and tarragon may be used instead of the chervil and parsley.

COOK'S TIP   The herbs should be visible through the pasta. Pass the sandwiched strips of dough through closely-set rollers on the pasta machine.

☐

OPPOSITE

HERB RAVIOLI
WITH CHICKEN
STOCK

---- SERVES 4 ----

LASAGNE

*Strips of home-made pasta, cooked
with beef, onion, mushrooms, wine and
tomato make for a very filling dish.*

Step 7

Step 8

Step 8

PASTA

□ 3 ½ cups all-purpose flour, sifted   □ 3 eggs, beaten   □ Salt

LASAGNE FILLING

□ 1 ⅓ lbs ground beef   □ 1 medium onion, chopped
□ 1 clove garlic, chopped   □ 2 cups chicken stock
□ 2 mushrooms, rinsed and chopped
□ ¼ cup white wine   □ ¼ cup butter
□ 1 tbsp tomato paste   □ Sprig thyme
□ 1 bay leaf   □ Salt and pepper
□ 4 tbsps grated Parmesan cheese

---

1. Make the dough by mixing together the flour, eggs and salt. Form into a ball, coat with a little flour and place in the refrigerator for 30 minutes.

2. Heat half of the butter in a frying pan and cook the onion and garlic until light brown.

3. Stir in the meat and mushrooms and cook for 2 minutes.

4. Deglaze the pan with the white wine, allow it to reduce and stir in 1 cup chicken stock. Add the thyme, bay leaf and tomato paste, season with salt and pepper and cook until the liquid has reduced by half. Remove the thyme and bay leaf.

5. Roll the dough out thinly or pass it through a pasta machine and cut into even-sized rectangular strips.

6. Cook the pasta strips for 1 minute in salted, boiling water, rinse under hot water and set aside to drain on a slightly damp tea towel.

7. Grease an ovenproof dish with the remaining butter and lay strips of pasta into the base.

8. Cover each layer of pasta with a layer of the meat sauce and continue layering until all the pasta and sauce has been used up.

9. Pour over the remaining chicken stock, sprinkle over the grated Parmesan cheese and cook in a moderately hot oven until the juices have almost entirely evaporated – approximately 40 minutes. Serve piping hot from the oven.

TIME   Preparation takes about 45 minutes and cooking takes approximately 50 minutes.

TIME SAVER   Using ready-made lasagne pasta will reduce preparation time considerably.

WATCHPOINT   Check the lasagne whilst it is cooking and add a little of the chicken stock if cooking time is not up and the sauce has already evaporated, or if the pasta becomes too dry or brown on top.

□

OPPOSITE

LASAGNE

—— SERVES 4 ——

FONTINA CHEESE RAVIOLI

*Try to buy Fontina cheese from an Italian food store if possible
for this fresh ravioli with Fontina stuffing. The cheese ravioli
are served in a sauce of reduced chicken stock and rosemary.*

Step 3

Step 5

Step 5

Step 6

☐

OPPOSITE

FONTINA CHEESE
RAVIOLI

☐ 5oz Fontina cheese   ☐ 1 tbsp chopped chives
☐ 2 cups all-purpose flour, sifted   ☐ 3 eggs
☐ 1 sprig rosemary
☐ 1½ cups chicken stock   ☐ Salt and pepper

1. Make the pasta dough by mixing together the flour, 2 eggs and
a good pinch of salt. Form into a ball and keep in the refrigerator
until needed.

2. Cut the cheese into small cubes and mix with the chives.

3. Roll the dough or pass it through the rollers of a pasta machine
and then lay the strips over a ravioli tray.

4. Beat the remaining egg and brush over the pasta with the help
of a small brush.

5. Place a little of the cheese mixture into each indent and then
cover with another strip of pasta.

6. Roll over the top of this second strip of pasta with a rolling pin
and remove the ravioli. Keep them to one side on a floured plate.

7. Set the stock and the rosemary to boil, season with salt and
pepper and cook the ravioli in this flavored stock for
approximately 2 minutes.

8. Remove the ravioli when they are cooked and keep them
warm.

9. Boil the sauce briskly to reduce it somewhat, remove the
rosemary and serve poured over the ravioli.

TIME   Preparation takes about 40 minutes and cooking time is
approximately 10 minutes.

SERVING IDEA   If you do not have a ravioli tray, cut the ravioli
into small shapes using a sharp knife once they have been stuffed
and the second strip of dough is in place and well stuck down.

COOK'S TIP   Flour the ravioli tray before placing in the first
strip.

WATCHPOINT   Brush the pasta well with the beaten egg and
make sure that the ravioli "packets" are well sealed before
cooking.

PASTA WITH FRESH BASIL SAUCE

*The fresh basil sauce is made by pounding
basil leaves with garlic, Parmesan and
olive oil using a pestle and mortar.*

Step 2

Step 3

☐ 1lb fresh pasta   ☐ 20 fresh basil leaves   ☐ 1 clove garlic
☐ 2 tbsps grated Parmesan   ☐ ¼ cup olive oil
☐ 2 tbsps butter   ☐ Salt and pepper

1. Cook the pasta in salted, boiling water. Drain, rinse and then set aside to drain well.

2. Pound the basil leaves in a mortar and pestle, then add the garlic and pound until well mixed.

3. Add the Parmesan and continue to pound.

4. Transfer the above to a large bowl and whisk in the olive oil.

5. Add the butter to the pasta, place over a gentle heat and add the basil sauce. Stir well with a wooden spoon, and season with salt and pepper. Serve as soon as the pasta is heated through completely.

TIME   Preparation takes about 25 minutes and cooking takes approximately 8 minutes.

VARIATION   The sauce can be made in a food processor by adding all the ingredients together and processing until smooth. This reduces the preparation time to about 3 minutes.

SERVING IDEA   Add pine nuts to the finished dish.

☐

OPPOSITE

PASTA WITH FRESH
BASIL SAUCE

——— SERVES 4 ———

FRESH PASTA WITH BASIL AND TOMATO SAUCE

*Fresh pasta with lots of finely chopped basil
is combined with a cooked tomato sauce
for a delicious and filling dish.*

☐ 1lb fresh pasta
☐ 3 tomatoes, skined, seeded and chopped
☐ 10 fresh basil leaves, finely chopped   ☐ 3 tbsps olive oil
☐ 1 clove garlic, chopped   ☐ Salt and pepper

1. Cook the pasta to your liking in salted, boiling water. Rinse under hot water and set aside to drain.

2. Heat the olive oil in a frying pan and cook the garlic, tomato, salt and pepper over a gentle heat for approximately 12 minutes, stirring frequently.

3. Stir the well drained pasta into the sauce, mix well and heat through completely.

4. Just before serving, stir in the finely chopped basil, check and adjust the seasoning and serve hot.

TIME   Preparation takes about 8 minutes and cooking takes approximately 25 minutes.

VARIATION   Add a finely chopped onion to the olive oil with the garlic, allow it to brown slightly, then add the tomato and continue cooking as above.

COOK'S TIP   Use really ripe tomatoes for this recipe.

☐

OPPOSITE

FRESH PASTA WITH
BASIL AND TOMATO
SAUCE

SERVES 4

SPINACH-STUFFED CANNELLONI

*A marvellous filling for cannelloni,
made with Mozzarella cheese, ham and spinach.
Absolutely delicious.*

Step 2

Step 3

Step 4

☐ 12 cannelloni
☐ 8oz spinach, washed and finely shredded
☐ 3 slices ham, cut into thin strips
☐ 8oz Mozzarella cheese, cut into small cubes
☐ 1 cup white sauce   ☐ 2 tbsps butter
☐ 3 tbsps grated Parmesan cheese   ☐ Pinch nutmeg
☐ Salt and pepper

1. Cook the cannelloni in salted boiling water, removing them when they are still quite firm (approximately 3 minutes). Rinse them in hot water and set aside to drain on a slightly damp tea towel.

2. Heat the butter in a frying pan and gently cook the spinach and the ham for 2 minutes.

3. Remove from the heat and stir in the Mozzarella cheese.

4. Fill each of the cannelloni with the above stuffing.

5. Lay the cannelloni in a lightly-greased ovenproof dish, pour over the white sauce and season with the nutmeg, salt and pepper.

6. Sprinkle over the Parmesan cheese and cook in a hot oven for 15 minutes. Serve piping hot.

TIME   Preparation takes about 25 minutes and cooking takes approximately 35 minutes.

VARIATION   Leftover cooked meat may be chopped finely and added to the stuffing.

WATCHPOINT   The topping should be lightly golden when cooked; if necessary, place under the broiler for a minute before serving.

☐

OPPOSITE

SPINACH-STUFFED
CANNELLONI

SERVES 4

CALABRIAN OYSTERS

*Oysters cooked in their shells and coated in
parsley, garlic, olive oil and breadcrumbs.*

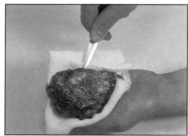

Step 1

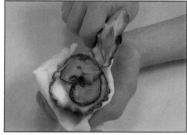

Step 1

☐ 16 large oysters, opened ☐ 2 tbsps finely chopped parsley
☐ 1 clove garlic, chopped ☐ 1 tbsp olive oil
☐ ¼ cup breadcrumbs ☐ Pepper

1. Using a small, sharp knife, remove the oysters from their shells.

2. Place each oyster back into a half shell with ¼ of its original juice.

3. Sprinkle over each oyster a little parsley, garlic and breadcrumbs.

4. Add a few drops of olive oil and a sprinkling of freshly ground pepper.

5. Cook the oysters for 10 minutes in a hot oven and then serve directly on removal from the oven.

TIME   Preparation takes about 20 minutes and cooking takes approximately 10 minutes.

SERVING IDEA   Serve with small cubes of fried bread.

COOK'S TIP   Use a thick tea towel to protect your hands when opening the oysters.

☐

OPPOSITE

CALABRIAN
OYSTERS

—— SERVES 4 ——

WHELK AND COCKLE SALAD

*Whelks prepared in a vegetable stock and cockles
cooked in white wine are served on a tossed salad
flavored with a tangy lemon vinaigrette dressing.*

Step 5

Step 5

Step 5

Step 5

☐ 32 large whelks   ☐ 1 carrot, sliced   ☐ 1 leek, sliced
☐ 1 onion, sliced   ☐ ¾ lb cockles   ☐ ¾ cup white wine
☐ 4 small servings of mixed fancy leaf lettuce, washed and dried
☐ Small bunch chives   ☐ Juice of 1 lemon
☐ ¼ cup olive oil   ☐ 1 sprig thyme   ☐ 1 bay leaf
☐ Salt and pepper

1. Wash the shellfish really well in lots of cold water. Brush with a small nail brush to remove any sand or grit. Change the water frequently, or rinse under cold, running water once you think they are clean.

2. Place the whelks in a saucepan of water with the carrot, leek and onion. Bring to the boil and then simmer gently for approximately 2 hours, checking for doneness after 2 hours. Cooking time will depend on the size of the whelks.

3. Place the cockles in a frying pan with the white wine, thyme and bay leaf. Cover, bring the contents to a brisk boil and cook until the shells open.

4. Remove from the heat when the shells are opened and allow to cool. Once they are cool enough to handle, remove the cockles from their shells and discard everything else.

5. When the whelks are cooked, set them aside to cool and then remove them from their shells. Pull off any black parts from the body of the whelk and also the muscle at the bottom of the body. The intestinal tract may also be removed, if desired.

6. Chop the chives finely and stir them into the lemon juice, olive oil, salt and pepper.

7. Toss the prepared lettuce, whelks and cockles in the sauce and serve on small individual plates.

TIME   Preparation takes about 40 minutes, cooling takes about 30 minutes and cooking time is approximately 2 hours.

SERVING IDEA   Keep a few whelk shells aside for decoration. Dry them and put a whelk back into each shell; add these to the tossed salad just before serving.

WATCHPOINT   Cooking of the whelks is a long job, but don't expect them to be soft after 2 hours; they are cooked when they are still slightly chewy and elastic.

☐

OPPOSITE

WHELK AND
COCKLE SALAD

———— SERVES 4 ————

GRILLED TUNA
WITH ROSEMARY

A quick and easy way of serving sumptuous fresh tuna steaks.

Step 1

Step 1

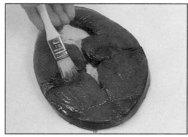

Step 2

□ 2 large tuna steaks   □ 1 tsp chopped rosemary
□ 2 tbsps breadcrumbs   □ 1 tbsp chopped parsley
□ 1 clove garlic, finely chopped   □ 2 tbsps olive oil
□ 2 lemons   □ Salt and pepper

1. Remove the bone from each tuna steak.

2. Brush the steaks on one side with oil and sprinkle over half of the parsley, rosemary, garlic, breadcrumbs, salt and pepper. Preheat a cast iron griddle or a heavy frying pan.

3. When the griddle or frying pan is really hot, wipe over a little oil with a paper towel and place on the tuna steaks, herbed side down.

4. Quickly brush the tops of the steaks with the remaining oil, and sprinkle over the remaining parsley, rosemary, garlic, breadcrumbs and a little salt and pepper. Turn the steaks to cook other side.

5. Cook the tuna to your liking. If using a griddle, give the steaks quarter turn on each side to give them a charred grid pattern.

6. Serve immediately, accompanied by lemon halves.

TIME   Preparation takes about 10 minutes and cooking takes approximately 8 to 12 minutes, depending on how well cooked you like your fish.

SERVING IDEA   Serve with a tossed green salad and mayonnaise.

COOK'S TIP   If the steaks are very thick, mark them on each side on the hot griddle and then transfer to a hot oven to finish cooking.

□

OPPOSITE

GRILLED TUNA
WITH ROSEMARY

STUFFED SARDINES

Fresh sardines filled with a delicious stuffing of anchovies, capers and spinach.

Step 3

Step 4

Step 4

- □ 12 sardines, washed, emptied and boned from the center
- □ 1 egg   □ ¼ lb spinach, cut into strips   □ 2 tsps capers
- □ 4 anchovy fillets in oil   □ 1 tbsp chopped parsley
- □ ½ cup breadcrumbs   □ 1 tbsp onion, chopped
- □ 2 tbsps olive oil   □ Salt and pepper

1. Chop together the anchovies and the capers.

2. Stir in the breadcrumbs and a little salt and pepper.

3. Mix the spinach with the egg, onion and parsley, and add to the above mixture. Stir well to mix the ingredients thoroughly.

4. Fill each of the sardines with the stuffing and place them upright in an ovenproof dish.

5. Pour over the olive oil and cook in a medium oven for approximately 15 minutes. Serve hot.

TIME   Preparation takes about 40 minutes and cooking takes approximately 15 to 20 minutes.

VARIATION   The spinach can be replaced with Swiss chard. Sprinkle over lots of grated Parmesan cheese just before cooking.

COOK'S TIP   Brush the fish with oil before placing them in the oven to prevent them from sticking together during cooking.

□

OPPOSITE

STUFFED SARDINES

SERVES 4

RED SNAPPER WITH VINAIGRETTE SAUCE

The fish fillets are served, either warm or cold, in a delicious vinaigrette sauce delicately flavored with fresh basil.

Step 2

Step 2

Step 2

☐ ¼ cup Xeres or wine vinegar
☐ 10 leaves fresh basil, cut into thin strips
☐ ½ cup olive oil   ☐ 2 tomatoes, seeded and diced
☐ 2 tbsps oil
☐ 6 red snapper, emptied, scaled and cut into fillets
☐ Salt and pepper

1. Mix together the vinegar, basil, salt, pepper and the olive oil. Stir in the diced tomato once the sauce is well mixed together.

2. In a frying pan, heat the oil and fry the fillets, skin side first. When fried on both sides, remove and drain on paper towels.

3. Place the fried fillets in a bowl, pour over the sauce and leave to marinate for at least 1 hour before serving.

TIME   Preparation takes about 25 minutes and cooking takes approximately 5 minutes.

COOK'S TIP   When frying the fillets, begin with the skin side first, so that they stay nice and flat.

VARIATION   Removing the fillets from red snapper is a delicate job. As an alternative, the fish can be emptied, scaled and fried whole, before taking slices off for marinating.

SERVING IDEA   This dish can be served cold or even chilled, straight from the refrigerator.

☐

OPPOSITE

RED SNAPPER
WITH
VINAIGRETTE
SAUCE

---- SERVES 4 ----

EEL IN RED WINE

Round slices of eel fried with onion and garlic and cooked in red wine and tomato sauce. Quick to prepare and cook, this is an impressive dish to serve at short notice.

Step 3

Step 4

Step 4

☐ 1¼ lbs eel, skinned   ☐ 2 onions, finely sliced
☐ 1 clove garlic, chopped   ☐ 1½ cups red wine
☐ 1 tsp sugar   ☐ 3 tbsps crushed tomato pulp
☐ ½ cup fish stock   ☐ 2 tbsps olive oil
☐ Salt and pepper

1. Cut the eel into medium-thick slices and season with salt and pepper.

2. Heat the oil and fry the onion and garlic for 1 minute.

3. Add the eel slices to the pan and seal on both sides.

4. Stir the wine and sugar into the pan, cook until the wine reduces somewhat, then add the tomato and the fish stock. Season with salt and pepper.

5. Transfer to an ovenproof dish and finish cooking in a medium oven for 15 minutes.

6. Remove the eel from the dish and, if the sauce is not very thick, pour it into a saucepan and thicken and reduce it over a high heat. Serve hot, with the sauce poured over.

TIME   Preparation takes about 20 minutes and cooking takes approximately 25 minutes.

VARIATION   Add a bouquet garni made up of thyme, bay leaf and parsley to the dish at Step 5.

COOK'S TIP   To make a milder-flavored sauce, boil the wine in a saucepan and ignite when boiling. Cool slightly, then add to the pan as above.

☐

OPPOSITE

EEL IN RED WINE

MUSSEL RISOTTO

To turn this risotto into a dish fit for the most sophisticated dinner party, all you need to do is press it into a round mold and then turn out and decorate with parsley.

Step 2

☐ 1 quart small mussels   ☐ 2 cups rice
☐ 1 shallot, chopped   ☐ ½ cup white wine
☐ 1 onion, chopped   ☐ ¼ cup butter
☐ Saffron (powdered variety)   ☐ Salt and pepper

1. Clean the mussels under plenty of running water, scraping and brushing off any sand and grit.

2. Place the clean mussels in a large saucepan with the shallot and the wine. Cook over a high heat until the mussels open.

3. Set the saucepan aside to allow the mussels to cool. Once they are cool, remove the mussels from their shells. Strain the cooking juices through a fine sieve which has been covered with a cheesecloth. Discard all but the juice and the mussels.

4. Melt the butter in a frying pan and gently fry the onion and the rice. Fry until the rice is transparent (approximately 1 minute) and then pour over the cooking juices made up to 3 cups with water. Stir in 2 to 3 pinches of saffron, just enough to slightly color the liquid.

5. Transfer to an ovenproof dish, season with salt and pepper and stir in the mussels. Cover and cook in a hot oven for approximately 20 minutes. Serve hot.

TIME   Preparation takes about 10 minutes and total cooking time is approximately 35 minutes.

WATCHPOINT   Do not add too much salt to the dish as the mussels give a rather salty flavor of their own.

COOK'S TIP   Spoon the cooked risotto into a round mold, then tip out onto a serving dish and decorate with fresh parsley.

☐

OPPOSITE

MUSSEL RISOTTO

—— SERVES 4 ——

TUSCAN-STYLE RED SNAPPER

A superb recipe for red snapper, whether served hot or cold.

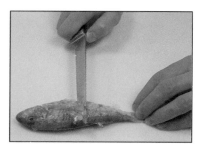

□ 4 tbsps olive oil
□ 8 small red snapper, gutted, scaled and cut into fillets
□ 1 shallot, chopped   □ ½ onion, finely chopped
□ 1 clove garlic, chopped
□ 6 large tomatoes, peeled, seeded and roughly chopped
□ 1 tsp chopped parsley   □ ½ tsp marjoram
□ 1 tsp sugar   □ 1 tbsp vinegar   □ Salt and pepper

1. Heat 2 tbsps olive oil in a frying pan and gently fry the shallot, onion, garlic and tomato. Stir well and cook for 2 minutes.

2. Stir into the contents of the pan the parsley, marjoram, sugar, salt and pepper. Cook for 30 minutes on a very low heat.

3. When the sauce is cooked, blend smooth with a hand mixer, adding the vinegar during blending, and set aside.

4. Heat the remaining oil in a frying pan, fry the fillets, skin side down first, and then pat them dry with paper towels.

5. Serve the fillets hot, warm or cold, with the sauce poured over.

TIME   Preparation takes about 30 minutes and cooking takes approximately 40 minutes.

SERVING IDEA   Serve with diced, sautéed green pepper.

□

OPPOSITE

TUSCAN-STYLE
RED SNAPPER

—— SERVES 4 ——

STUFFED SQUID

Filled with a smooth, tangy fish stuffing,
the squid are steam cooked, sliced and
served with a lemon-flavored vinaigrette.

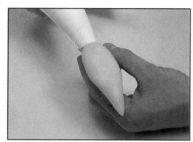

Step 5

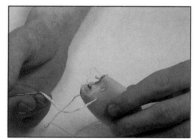

Step 5

☐ 9oz fish flesh   ☐ 1 egg   ☐ 4 anchovy fillets in oil
☐ 2 tbsps light cream
☐ 8 medium squid, emptied and washed
☐ 1 tbsp heavy cream
☐ 1 lettuce, washed, dried and broken into small pieces
☐ 2 tomatoes, sliced or cubed   ☐ 1 tbsp lemon juice
☐ 2 tbsps olive oil   ☐ Salt and pepper

1. Place the fish flesh, egg, anchovies, light cream, salt and pepper in a mixer and blend until smooth. Place in the refrigerator for 30 minutes.

2. Cook the squid in a steamer for 10 minutes. When cooked, rinse in cold water and set aside to drain.

3. Pass the fish mixture through a fine sieve, pushing it through with the back of a spoon.

4. Using a spatula, mix the heavy cream into the fish stuffing.

5. Fill the squid with the fish stuffing and then tie up the ends using a needle and thread.

6. Place the stuffed squid in a steamer and cook for 15 minutes.

7. Mix together the lemon juice, olive oil, salt and pepper and toss the lettuce in this dressing.

8. Place a little salad on 4 plates, dot over the tomato and serve with the stuffed squid, either hot or cold, sliced into rounds.

TIME   Preparation takes about 1 hour and cooking takes approximately 30 minutes.

VARIATION   A little finely chopped garlic or cooked, diced vegetables mixed with herbs may be added to the dressing.

COOK'S TIP   Make sure that the squid are very well dried on the inside, wiping out any excess moisture with kitchen paper before stuffing This ensures that the stuffing, when cooked, sticks to the sides of the squid.

☐

OPPOSITE

STUFFED SQUID

SERVES 4

MARINATED SARDINES

Cooked sardines in a vinegar marinade
flavored with onions and pine nuts.

Step 1

Step 1

Step 1

☐ 20 equal-sized sardines ☐ Handful pine nuts
☐ 2 large onions, finely sliced ☐ 1 tbsp olive oil
☐ 1 cup distilled vinegar ☐ Flour for dredging
☐ ¼ cup oil ☐ Salt and pepper

1. Remove the heads from the sardines, then gut and bone the fish.

2. Dredge the fillets in the flour and season with plenty of salt and pepper.

3. Heat the cooking oil in a frying pan, fry the fillets on both sides and drain on paper towels.

4. Heat the olive oil in a frying pan and gently fry the onions and pine nuts for a few minutes.

5. Deglaze the pan with the vinegar, and continue cooking for 30 seconds. Remove from the heat and set aside for a moment.

6. Place the sardines in a large dish, putting a little of the onion mixture between each fillet.

7. Pour over the warm vinegar and leave to marinate in a cool place for a few days.

TIME Preparation takes about 1 hour and cooking takes about 10 minutes.

VARIATION Use fresh anchovies instead of sardines.

COOK'S TIP Fry the sardines quickly on both sides; they do not have to be cooked through thoroughly.

☐

OPPOSITE

MARINATED
SARDINES

––––––––– SERVES 4 –––––––––

CHICKEN WITH
TOMATO SAUCE

*Chicken cooked in the frying pan and served
with a tasty wine and tomato sauce.*

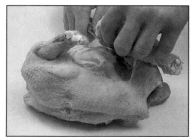

Step 1

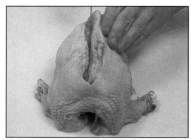

Step 1

Step 1

☐ 1 large chicken ☐ 1 cup red wine
☐ 1 onion, chopped ☐ 2 tbsps oil
☐ 1 cup tomato juice
☐ 2 strips bacon, chopped into small pieces
☐ 1 cup chicken stock ☐ 1 sprig tarragon
☐ 12 baby onions ☐ Salt and pepper

1. Joint the chicken into 2 leg and 2 breast portions, retaining the carcase and wings to use for stock.

2. In a saucepan, bring the red wine to the boil and then ignite; this helps to remove the acidity of the wine. Remove from the heat.

3. Heat the oil in a frying pan and brown the chicken pieces on all sides to seal.

4. Add the chopped onion to the chicken, cook for 1 minute and then deglaze the pan by pouring in the red wine.

5. Allow the liquid to reduce somewhat over a high heat and then stir in the tomato juice, bacon, chicken stock, tarragon and the baby onions.

6. Stir well, season with salt and pepper and continue to cook on a moderate heat, stirring from time to time, for approximately 30 minutes.

7. When the sauce coats the back of a spoon, remove the chicken and the baby onions and push the sauce through a very fine sieve.

8. Put all the ingredients back on a moderate heat to heat through thoroughly and then serve immediately.

TIME   Preparation takes about 25 minutes and cooking time is approximately 45 minutes.

COOK'S TIP   To make your own chicken stock, boil the bones in a large saucepan with carrot, onion, leek, herbs, salt and pepper, until the stock is well flavored. Strain through a fine sieve and keep in the fridge for up to 3 days.

COOK'S TIP   Soaking the baby onions in warm water for 10 minutes makes them easier to peel.

☐

OPPOSITE

CHICKEN WITH
TOMATO SAUCE

SERVES 4

OLIVE-STUFFED RABBIT MEAT

*Saddle of rabbit with olive stuffing
cooked in a tomato-based sauce.*

Step 1

Step 3

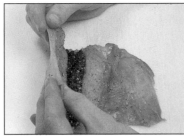

Step 4

Step 5

☐

OPPOSITE

OLIVE-STUFFED
RABBIT MEAT

☐ 2 saddles rabbit ☐ ½ tsp chopped rosemary
☐ Salt and pepper ☐ 3 tbsps chopped olives
☐ 1 clove garlic, chopped
☐ 3 large tomatoes, peeled, seeded and chopped
½ cup tomato juice ☐ ½ cup chicken stock
☐ 2 tbsps olive oil

---

1. Remove the bones from the 2 saddles, taking care not to pierce the meat

2. Sprinkle the inside of the meat with the rosemary, salt and pepper.

3. Mix together the chopped garlic and the olives. Spread this stuffing down the center of each saddle.

4. Roll up the meat, taking care to roll tightly and neatly.

5. Secure the 2 rolls of stuffed meat with thin kitchen string.

6. Heat the olive oil in a frying pan and briskly seal the rolls on all sides until golden brown.

7. Add the tomatoes, stock and tomato juice to the pan, stirring well to mix.

8. Season with salt and pepper, cover and cook on a moderate heat for 20 minutes. Check the level of the liquid in the pan frequently, stirring and shaking the ingredients from time to time.

9. After 20 minutes, remove the rolls to a hot plate and allow the remaining sauce to reduce and thicken.

10. Cut the rolls into slices and serve on the tomato sauce.

TIME   Preparation takes about 30 minutes and cooking takes approximately 45 minutes.

VARIATION   For the stuffing, use a mixture of green and black olives, or just green olives.

WATCHPOINT   Boning the saddles is a delicate job. The meat should not have any holes at all, but should you make a small hole, patch it with a piece of meat.

ROAST QUAIL

Delicious crisply roasted quail flavored with rosemary.

Step 1

☐ 4 large quail, emptied ☐ 1 tbsp chopped rosemary
☐ 1 tbsp oil ☐ Salt and pepper

1. Cut off the ends of the wings and the legs. Rinse the quail under cold running water.
2. Sprinkle the insides of the quail evenly with the rosemary.
3. Sprinkle salt and pepper over the rosemary.
4. Tie the quail up neatly with thin kitchen string.
5. Heat the oil in a frying pan and seal the quail on all sides.
6. Transfer to a hot oven and cook until crisp and golden.

TIME   Preparation takes about 10 minutes and total cooking time is approximately 30 minutes, depending on the size of the bird.

COOK'S TIP   Serve the quail slightly pink; the meat becomes dry if overcooked.

SERVING IDEA   Serve the quail on a bed of spaghetti with fresh basil.

☐

OPPOSITE

ROAST QUAIL

CHICKEN RISOTTO

*A tasty rice dish delicately flavored
with celery, onion and carrot.*

Step 1

Step 2

□ ⅞ cup long grain rice
□ 2 chicken legs, boned and the meat cut into small dice
□ 2 sticks celery, cut into small dice
□ 1 carrot, cut into small dice
□ 1 white onion, cut into small dice   □ 1 tbsp butter
□ Salt and pepper

1. Heat the butter in a casserole and gently fry the onion, celery and carrot for 2 minutes.

2. Add the diced chicken, stir well and cook for 1 minute.

3. Add the rice, stir well and cook until the rice is transparent.

4. Pour over water to 3 times the volume of the rice used. Season with salt and pepper.

5. Cover and cook in a hot oven 400°F, for approximately 18 minutes. Serve hot.

TIME   Preparation takes approximately 10 minutes and cooking takes about 25 minutes.

VARIATION   Use turkey breast instead of the chicken.

COOK'S TIP   Use chicken stock instead of water; this will improve the flavor of the rice.

□

OPPOSITE

CHICKEN RISOTTO

SERVES 4

MOZZARELLA CHICKEN BREASTS

Chicken breasts coated in breadcrumbs and stuffed with tasty Mozzarella cheese.

Step 1

Step 2

Step 5

☐ 4 chicken breasts   ☐ 2 tbsps chopped parsley
☐ 1 shallot, chopped   ☐ 4 large slices Mozzarella cheese
☐ 1 egg, beaten   ☐ 2 cups fresh breadcrumbs
☐ 3 tbsps oil   ☐ 2 tbsps butter   ☐ Flour for dredging
☐ Salt and pepper

1. Open the breasts out, but do not cut them in two.

2. Sprinkle the insides with salt, pepper, parsley, shallot and add a slice of Mozzarella.

3. Ease back into place the top of the chicken breast.

4. Sprinkle the flour all over the stuffed breasts.

5. Dip the floured breasts in the beaten egg.

6. Finally dip the breasts in the breadcrumbs, pressing the crumbs well into the egg coating.

7. Heat the oil and butter in a frying pan and seal the breasts on all sides. Allow them to color up to a nice golden brown.

8. Transfer to an ovenproof dish and finish cooking in a moderate oven for approximately 15 minutes.

9. Serve hot, either whole or sliced.

TIME   Preparation takes about 25 minutes and cooking takes approximately 25 minutes.

SERVING IDEA   Serve the breasts with a quarter of lemon; lemon juice enlivens the flavor of the chicken.

COOK'S TIP   Brushing a little beaten egg on the insides of the breasts helps them seal during frying, thus preventing the cheese from escaping during cooking.

☐

OPPOSITE

MOZZARELLA
CHICKEN BREASTS

WALNUT RABBIT

*A delicious concoction of walnuts, olives,
white wine, stock, mustard and fresh cream.*

Step 1

Step 2

Step 3

☐ 1 rabbit, boned and the meat cut into small pieces
☐ 1 onion, finely chopped ☐ 1 small stick celery, finely chopped
☐ 15 green olives, stoned and finely chopped
☐ 15 walnuts, shelled ☐ 2 cups white wine ☐ 2 tbsps olive oil
☐ 2 cups chicken stock ☐ ½ tsp mustard
☐ 2 tbsps heavy cream ☐ Salt and pepper

1. Heat the oil in a flameproof casserole and gently fry the onion and celery until tender.

2. Add the rabbit meat, stir and then add the olives and walnuts. Cook for 5 minutes, stirring frequently.

3. Pour in the wine and cook over a high heat until the wine has almost evaporated.

4. Pour over the stock and add a little water to cover. Season with salt and pepper, and cook on a low heat until the rabbit is tender and the juices somewhat reduced.

5. Remove the meat and whisk in the mustard and cream; do not allow the sauce to boil. Replace the meat, stir and serve.

TIME   Preparation takes about 25 minutes and cooking takes approximately 1 hour and 30 minutes.

WATCHPOINT   The mustard should not be allowed to boil, otherwise it becomes grainy.

VARIATION   Make a stock using the rabbit bones and adding a few vegetables. Use this to replace the chicken stock.

☐

OPPOSITE

WALNUT RABBIT

— SERVES 4 —

CHICKEN BREASTS WITH HOT PEPPER SAUCE

Tasty chicken breasts with onion, hot pepper sauce, garlic, chicken stock and white wine.

Step 2

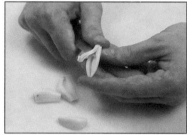
Step 2

Step 2

☐ 4 chicken breasts ☐ 1 clove garlic, finely chopped
☐ 2 tsps hot pepper sauce ☐ 1 large onion, chopped
☐ ¾ cup chicken stock ☐ 1 tbsp olive oil
☐ ¼ cup white wine ☐ Salt and pepper

1. Heat the oil in a frying pan, add the chicken breasts and cook them gently on all sides over a gentle heat until just colored.

2. To prepare the garlic, peel the clove and cut it in two lengthwise. Remove the green central shoot and finely chop the two halves. Add the garlic, onion and hot pepper sauce to the pan and stir well.

3. Pour over the wine, increase the heat and cook until the wine has evaporated.

4. Reduce the heat and stir in the stock. Season with salt and pepper and allow to cook through, covered, for 10 minutes.

5. Remove the breasts to a preheated plate and raise the heat to reduce and thicken the sauce.

6. Pour a little sauce over each chicken breast and serve.

TIME   Preparation takes about 5 minutes and cooking takes approximately 30 minutes.

VARIATION   Sprinkle over lots of freshly chopped chives just before serving.

COOK'S TIP   Adjust the quantity of hot pepper sauce to taste. If unavailable, improvise by mixing a few drops Tabasco with a teaspoon or two of tomato paste.

☐

OPPOSITE

CHICKEN BREASTS
WITH
HOT PEPPER SAUCE

--- SERVES 4 ---

QUAIL SALAD

Quail meat served on a mixed green salad with cubes of fried bread and a delicious sauce.

Step 1

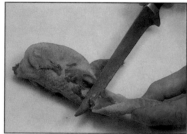

Step 1

Step 1

☐ 4 fresh quail   ☐ 4 slices of white bread   ☐ 1 tbsp olive oil
☐ 5 tbsps oil   ☐ ½ carrot, chopped   ☐ 1 shallot, chopped
☐ Salt and pepper   ☐ Vinegar
☐ 4 small servings of mixed green salad

1. Remove the legs and the breast meat from the quail. Draw the birds if this has not been done by the butcher and discard all the entrails.

2. Wash the salad greens and dry the leaves well.

3. Heat 1 tbsps oil in a pan and add the wings and the carcasses. Brown well and cover with 1 cup water. Add the carrot and the shallot, and season with salt and pepper. Leave on a high heat until the stock has reduced by half.

4. Strain the stock through a fine sieve and discard the bones.

5. Put the stock back on a high heat and cook until it becomes quite syrupy. Remove from the heat and allow to cool.

6. Once the stock has cooled, stir in the olive oil and a drop of vinegar. Stir well and set aside.

7. Cut the sliced bread into small cubes. Heat 2 tbsps of oil in a frying pan and fry the cubes on all sides. Drain on kitchen paper when golden.

8. Season the quail meat and legs with lots of salt and pepper and sauté in the remaining oil until cooked through completely.

9. Serve the legs and quail meat on a bed of salad with the sauce poured over.

TIME   Preparation takes about 10 minutes and total cooking time is approximately 40 minutes.

VARIATION   Add a little chopped shallot to the mixed salad.

COOK'S TIP   When cooking the quail breasts in the oil, begin skin side down and turn often to prevent the meat from drying out.

☐

OPPOSITE

QUAIL SALAD

SERVES 4

ROSEMARY CHICKEN SURPRISE

Chicken meat stuffed with chicken liver, flavored with rosemary and gently braised in rich chicken stock.

Step 3

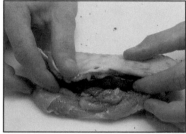

Step 3

Step 3

☐ 4 chicken legs, boned   ☐ 4 chicken livers
☐ 3 tbsps rosemary   ☐ 2 cups rich chicken stock
☐ ¼ cup butter   ☐ Salt and pepper

1. Cut any veins from the chicken livers and rinse them in plenty of cold water.

2. Spread the chicken meat on a work surface, skin side down. Sprinkle the inside of the meat with salt, pepper and 2 tbsps rosemary.

3. Place a chicken liver over the seasoning, roll the meat tightly around the liver and secure well with kitchen string. Do this for all 4 pieces of meat.

4. Heat the chicken stock with the remaining rosemary and add the chicken rolls. Cover and simmer gently for 20 minutes.

5. Remove the chicken rolls and keep them warm.

6. Place the saucepan back on a high heat and allow the sauce to reduce and thicken.

7. Reduce the heat to very low and whisk in the butter, piece, by piece.

8. Cut the rolls into slices and serve on a bed of spaghetti with the sauce poured over.

TIME   Preparation takes about 15 minutes and cooking takes approximately 45 minutes.

SERVING IDEA   Use any type of pasta as an accompaniment to this dish.

WATCHPOINT   Do not allow the sauce to boil while adding the butter, nor after the butter has been added.

☐

OPPOSITE

ROSEMARY
CHICKEN SURPRISE

RABBIT AND LIVER SURPRISE

*Stuffed and marinated rabbit thighs
simmered in a tasty stock make for
a deliciously different evening meal.*

Step 1

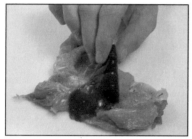

Step 2

Step 4

☐ 4 rabbit thighs   ☐ 2 rabbit livers   ☐ 1 tsp chopped sage
☐ 4 juniper berries   ☐ 3 tbsps olive oil
☐ 1 tsp chopped rosemary   ☐ 1 cup chicken stock
☐ Salt and pepper

1. Bone the rabbit thighs, keeping the meat in one piece.

2. Cut the livers in half and place one piece on each thigh.

3. Roll up the thighs and secure with thin kitchen string.

4. Mix together the rosemary, sage, juniper berries and the olive oil in a large bowl and add the rabbit thighs, leaving them to marinate in the mixture for an hour.

5. Heat half of the marinade in a frying pan and seal the meat briskly on all sides.

6. Pour off the oil from the frying pan, pour over the stock, cover and simmer gently for approximately 25 minutes.

7. When cooked, season with salt and pepper, cut in slices and serve on a preheated dish with the cooking juices poured over.

TIME   Preparation takes about 15 minutes, marinating time is 1 hour and cooking takes approximately 35 minutes.

VARIATION   If rabbit bones and trimmings are available, make your own rabbit stock for this recipe.

WATCHPOINT   Should the juices evaporate too quickly during cooking, add a little more stock or water to the pan.

☐

OPPOSITE

RABBIT AND LIVER
SURPRISE

—— SERVES 4 ——

COLD CHICKEN
SICILIAN STYLE

*Chilled caper-stuffed chicken served with
potatoes and a basil-flavored mayonnaise.*

Step 5

Step 5

Step 6

□ 4 chicken legs, boned
□ 2 large, good quality potatoes, steam cooked and peeled
□ 2 tbsps capers   □ 5 basil leaves, cut into very thin strips
□ 1 tbsp parsley   □ 1 egg yolk   □ ½ tsp mustard
□ 1 cup olive oil   □ Salt and pepper

1. Season the inside of the meat with plenty of salt and pepper.

2. Sprinkle 1 tbsp of capers over the seasoned meat, roll tightly and neatly, then secure with kitchen string.

3. Steam-cook these rolls for approximately 10 to 15 minutes, depending on their thickness.

4. Allow the rolls to cool and then cut them into round slices.

5. Prepare the mayonnaise by whisking together the egg yolk and the mustard. Add the olive oil drop by drop, whisking continuously until the oil has been used up.

6. Season the mayonnaise with salt, pepper and add the remaining capers, the basil and parsley.

7. Cut the potatoes into slices. Serve the potatoes and chicken with the mayonnaise dotted over.

TIME   Preparation takes about 25 minutes, cooking takes approximately 15 minutes and chiling time (the chicken, potatoes and mayonnaise should all be slightly chilled for this dish) approximately 20 minutes.

COOK'S TIP   Make the mayonnaise the day before use and keep it in the refrigerator, thus enabling it to absorb the flavors of the capers, basil and parsley.

Copyright © Frédéric Lebain

□

OPPOSITE

COLD CHICKEN
SICILIAN STYLE

————— SERVES 4 —————

MUTTON CHOPS IN RICH SAUCE

*Mutton cooked in a tasty stock thickened
and enriched with egg yolk.*

☐ 4 mutton chops (from the neck) ☐ 2 slices Parma ham
☐ ½ onion, sliced ☐ 1 clove garlic, chopped ☐ 1 bay leaf
☐ 1 sprig thyme ☐ ½ cup white wine ☐ 1 egg yolk
☐ Juice of ½ lemon ☐ 2 tbsps olive oil
☐ Flour for dredging ☐ Salt and pepper

Step 2

Step 3

Step 5

Step 6

1. Season the chops with salt and pepper and toss them in the flour, shaking off any excess.

2. Heat the oil and fry the chops on all sides to seal and brown.

3. Cut the ham into small dice and add them to the pan with the chops.

4. Add the onion and garlic to the pan and cook for 1 minute.

5. Deglaze the pan with the wine and keep on the heat until the wine has almost completely evaporated.

6. Pour in sufficient water to cover, and add the thyme, bay leaf, salt and pepper. Cook for 1 hour, stirring from time to time.

7. Whisk together the egg yolk and the lemon juice.

8. Remove the meat from the pan and stir the egg yolk and lemon juice into the pan juices, stirring continuously over a very gentle heat until the sauce thickens.

9. Take off the heat, remove the sprig of thyme and the bay leaf, and replace the meat.

TIME   Preparation takes about 10 minutes and cooking takes approximately 1 hour and 10 minutes.

VARIATION   If less of a garlic flavor is preferred, cut the clove of garlic in half and add without chopping. Remove the halves at the end of Step 6.

SERVING IDEA   Sprinkle over lots of parsley just before serving.

☐

OPPOSITE

MUTTON CHOPS IN
RICH SAUCE

SERVES 4

CARPACCIO WITH FRESH BASIL

*Thin slices of beef served raw with olive oil,
lemon juice, garlic and lots of fresh basil.*

Step 1

Step 1

☐ 1lb beef fillet   ☐ 2 cloves garlic, finely chopped
☐ 10 fresh basil leaves   ☐ 1 squeeze lemon juice
☐ 2 tbsp olive oil   ☐ Salt and pepper

1. Slice the meat thinly and spread out on a serving plate.

2. Mix together the olive oil, garlic and lemon juice.

3. Cut the basil leaves lengthwise into thin strips and add them to the oil mixture.

4. Brush the slices of meat with the oil, season with salt and pepper and arrange them on 4 small individual plates.

5. Allow to marinate for at least 10 minutes and serve at room temperature.

TIME   Preparation takes about 30 minutes.

COOK'S TIP   Placing the meat in the freezer for a couple of hours makes it much easier to slice thinly.

WATCHPOINT   The slices of beef must be very thin if they are to marinate quickly.

☐

OPPOSITE

CARPACCIO WITH
FRESH BASIL

—— SERVES 4 ——

ESCALOPES WITH CHEESE

Delicious veal rolls with a cheese and ham filling.

Step 1

Step 2

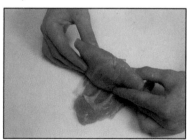

Step 3

□ 4 slices Parma ham
□ 8 slices Fontina, Cheddar or other soft cheese
□ 4 veal escalopes   □ 1 egg, beaten
□ 2 cups breadcrumbs   □ 3 tbsps oil   □ 2 tbsps butter
□ Flour for dredging   □ Salt and pepper

1. Flatten the escalopes between 2 sheets of plastic wrap, gently tapping them with the flat side of a long knife. Remove the plastic wrap.

2. Place a slice of ham over each escalope and then 2 pieces of cheese.

3. Roll the escalopes up firmly, so that the cheese and ham are well covered. Season with salt and pepper.

4. Roll the escalopes in the flour and then dip them in the beaten egg.

5. Shake off any excess egg and roll in the breadcrumbs, making sure they are well covered.

6. Heat the oil and butter together and fry the escalopes until nicely crisp and golden brown.

7. Transfer to an ovenproof dish and finish cooking in a medium oven. Serve hot.

TIME   Preparation takes about 30 minutes and cooking takes approximately 30 minutes.

VARIATION   Italian Fontina cheese is ideal for this recipe, although other soft cheeses may be used to substitute if unavailable.

WATCHPOINT   Do not let the fat get too hot when browning the escalopes otherwise the breadcrumbs may burn.

□

OPPOSITE

ESCALOPES
WITH CHEESE

—— SERVES 4 ——

OSSO BUCO WITH
ALMOND MARSALA

Everybody has tasted osso buco, but the addition of Marsala
flavored with almonds really brings this dish to life.

Step 1

Step 1

Step 2

▢ 4 thick slices of veal knuckle (with the bone) ▢ 1 onion, sliced
▢ 1 clove garlic, chopped
▢ ½ cup almond flavored Marsala
▢ 2 cups chicken stock
▢ ⅓ cup crushed tomato pulp ▢ 1 bay leaf
▢ 2 tbsps olive oil ▢ Salt and pepper

1. Heat the oil and gently fry the onions, garlic and the slices of veal until slightly colored.

2. Remove the excess fat with paper towels and deglaze the pan with the Marsala. Allow to reduce a little and then stir in the stock, tomato pulp and the bay leaf.

3. Pour over enough water to cover the meat. Season with salt and pepper and cook until the meat is tender and cooked through – about 1½-2 hours.

4. Serve hot with the sauce poured over.

TIME   Preparation takes 5 minutes and cooking takes approximately 2 hours.

VARIATION   If almond-flavored Marsala is not available, use classic Marsala instead.

COOK'S TIP   For a slightly more refined sauce, remove the meat and the bay leaf, blend the sauce smooth in a blender and then serve poured over the meat.

Copyright © Frédéric Lebain

▢

OPPOSITE

OSSO BUCO WITH
ALMOND MARSALA

——— SERVES 4 ———

PIEDMONT BEEF CASSEROLE

Sliced beef, smoked sausage and
vegetables served in a rich sauce.

Step 3

Step 3

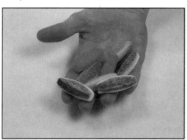

Step 3

☐ 1lb lean shoulder of beef
☐ 1 large smoked sausage (or a few small ones)
☐ ½ lb joint veal (knuckle)   ☐ 3 carrots   ☐ 2 zucchini
☐ ½ leek, thinly sliced   ☐ 1 onion, stuck with 1 clove
☐ 4 juniper berries   ☐ 1 cup chicken stock
☐ 1 bay leaf   ☐ 1 bouquet garni   ☐ Salt and pepper

1. Heat the stock in a large flameproof casserole, add an equal quantity of water and the meats (beef, sausage and the veal joint). Add 1 carrot, cut into thin rounds, the leek, onion, juniper berries, bay leaf and the bouquet garni.

2. Season with salt and pepper, add water to completely cover, and simmer for 2 ½ hours.

3. Meanwhile, cut the remaining carrots and the zucchini into oval shapes and steam them for a few minutes – they should still be quite crisp.

4. When the casserole is cooked, remove the meat and cut it into thin slices. Place the meat on a warmed serving dish.

5. Cut the sausage into rounds and the meat and fat off the joint into small cubes.

6. Strain the juices into a clean saucepan through a very fine sieve. Add the steamed vegetables to the pan and heat through.

7. Serve the vegetables around the cut meats, with the juices poured over.

TIME   Preparation takes about 30 minutes and cooking takes approximately 2 hours and 45 minutes.

COOK'S TIP   Slice the beef thinly before serving.

SERVING IDEA   Serve with creamed potato and a green vegetable, such as broccoli.

☐

OPPOSITE

PIEDMONT BEEF
CASSEROLE

—— SERVES 4 ——

LAMB WITH FENNEL

*A tasty lamb and fennel casserole flavored
with white wine and lemon juice.*

Step 2

Step 2

□ 1½ lbs leg of lamb   □ ¼ lb wild fennel
□ 2 onions, finely sliced   □ ½ cup white wine
□ 3 tbsps olive oil   □ 1 egg yolk   □ ½ lemon
□ 1 tbsp water   □ Salt and pepper

1. Cut the meat into cubes and season with salt and pepper.

2. Cut the fennel into rounds and fry gently with the onion and meat in the olive oil until slightly colored.

3. Deglaze the pan with the white wine and allow the wine to reduce somewhat before covering the ingredients with water.

4. Bring to the boil, cover, reduce the heat and simmer gently for approximately 1 hour and 45 minutes. Check the level of the liquid during cooking, and add water as necessary

5. Meanwhile, beat together the egg yolk, 1 tbsp water and the juice of ½ a lemon.

6. When the casserole is cooked and the meat quite tender, remove the meat and, over a low heat, whisk the egg yolk mixture into the sauce, whisking continuously until the mixture thickens

7. Put the meat back into the sauce and serve hot.

TIME   Preparation takes about 10 minutes and cooking takes approximately 1 hour and 50 minutes.

SERVING IDEA   Serve with braised fennel bulbs.

VARIATION   Use regular fennel instead of the wild variety.

WATCHPOINT   The sauce should be thickened over a very low heat, otherwise the egg yolk will coagulate and the sauce will become 'grainy'.

□

OPPOSITE

LAMB WITH
FENNEL

BEEF IN BAROLO

A delightfully rich beef stew cooked in a wine marinade.

Step 1

Step 1

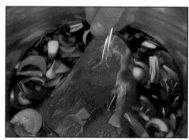
Step 1

☐ 2lbs silverside beef   ☐ 1 carrot, sliced   ☐ 1 onion, sliced
☐ ½ leek, sliced   ☐ 1 bay leaf   ☐ 1 sprig rosemary
☐ 1 sprig thyme   ☐ 2 tsps tomato paste
☐ 3 tbsps olive oil   ☐ 2 cloves garlic
☐ 1 bottle Barolo wine   ☐ 2 cups water or beef stock
☐ Salt and pepper   ☐ 5 peppercorns

1. Mix together the carrot, onion, leek, thyme, rosemary, bay leaf, garlic, peppercorns, a little ground pepper, tomato paste and the wine. Add the meat and marinate overnight.

2. Drain the meat, heat the olive oil and seal the meat on all sides until lightly browned.

3. Tip out excess fat and deglaze with the marinade. Pour over 2 cups of water or beef stock. Season with salt and pepper and simmer gently for 2 hours. Test the meat for tenderness and continue cooking if necessary, adding more water if required.

4. Cut the beef into slices, strain the sauce and serve with the sauce poured over.

TIME   Preparation takes about 5 minutes, plus overnight marinating, and cooking takes up to 3 hours.

COOK'S TIP   If the joint is thick, cut it in two so that it marinates thoroughly.

☐

OPPOSITE

BEEF IN BAROLO

—— SERVES 4 ——

SHOULDER OF VEAL
WITH TRUFFLES

Veal cooked with bacon and truffles in a wine-flavored sauce.

Step 4

Step 5

Step 5

☐ 1¼ lbs shoulder of veal, cut into cubes ☐ 1 onion, sliced ☐ 1 thick strip smoked bacon ☐ 2 medium truffles ☐ ¼ cup white wine ☐ 1 tbsp oil ☐ 2 tbsps butter ☐ Salt and pepper

1. Cut the bacon into small pieces.

2. Grate the truffles finely onto a plate.

3. Heat the oil and butter together and gently fry the onion and bacon for a few minutes.

4. Add the meat and allow to cook until browned all over.

5. Tip out any excess fat, deglaze the pan with the wine and allow it to evaporate almost completely. Season with salt and pepper, pour over water to cover and cook for approximately 45 minutes, or until the sauce reduces to just below the level of the meat.

6. Stir in the grated truffle, mix well and serve.

TIME   Preparation takes about 15 minutes and cooking takes approximately 1 hour.

VARIATION   Replace the bacon with smoked ham.

WATCHPOINT   The meat should be very tender when cooked. If necessary, add more water when the level drops, and continue cooking until ready.

☐

OPPOSITE

SHOULDER OF
VEAL WITH
TRUFFLES

─────── SERVES 4 ───────

HERBY PORK CHOPS

Pork chops flavored with garlic and parsley,
and served with sautéed potatoes.

Step 1

Step 1

Step 2

☐ 4 pork chops   ☐ 2 cloves garlic, chopped
☐ 4 tbsps chopped parsley   ☐ 4 large good quality potatoes
☐ 4 tbsps oil   ☐ 2 nuts butter   ☐ Salt and pepper

1. Bone the chops and season with plenty of salt and pepper.

2. Sprinkle the garlic and parsley over each of the chops, pressing well into the meat. Place the meat in the refrigerator until needed at Step 5.

3. Peel the potatoes and cut them into thin slices.

4. Heat together 2 tbsps oil and 1 nut of butter. Sauté the potatoes, adding any leftover garlic and parsley to the pan, until cooked through.

5. Fry the pork chops in the remaining oil and butter, browning them on all sides, and then finish cooking in a medium oven until cooked through.

6. Serve the chops hot with the sautéed potatoes.

TIME   Preparation takes about 30 minutes and cooking takes 35 minutes.

SERVING IDEA   Serve with a sauce of crushed tomato pulp warmed through and well seasoned with salt and pepper.

VARIATION   If you like lots of garlic, increase the quantity to 3 cloves, finely chopped.

☐

OPPOSITE

HERBY PORK
CHOPS

—— SERVES 4 ——

TUSCANY BEEF

Beef gently cooked in red wine and
flavored with rosemary and tomato.

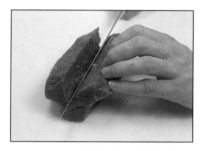

☐ 2lbs braising steak, cut into small cubes
☐ 1 clove garlic, chopped
☐ ½ tsp chopped rosemary
☐ 2 cups red wine   ☐ 2 tbsps tomato paste
☐ 3 tbsps olive oil   ☐ Flour for dredging
☐ Salt and pepper

1. Toss the meat cubes in the flour.

2. Heat the oil in a flameproof casserole, add the garlic, meat and rosemary. Fry on all sides until the meat is well browned.

3. Deglaze the casserole with the red wine and then pour in enough water to cover the meat.

4. Stir in the tomato paste, season with salt and pepper, cover and simmer gently for approximately 2 hours. Check the meat for tenderness and remove from the heat when cooked through. Serve hot.

TIME   Preparation takes about 5 minutes and cooking time can be up to 2½ hours.

SERVING IDEA   Serve with plain boiled rice or steamed potatoes.

WATCHPOINT   Check the level of the liquid during cooking and add water if necessary.

☐

OPPOSITE

TUSCANY BEEF

MILANESE RISOTTO

This rice risotto is cooked with red wine, stock and beef marrow. It is a tasty recipe that will surprise guests with its originality.

Step 2

Step 5

☐ 2 cups rice ☐ 2 marrow bones
☐ ½ onion, chopped ☐ ½ cup red wine
☐ 2 ½ cups chicken stock
☐ ¼ cup butter ☐ 2 pinches powdered saffron
☐ Salt and pepper

1. Cook the marrow bones in salted, boiling water for 15 minutes.

2. Remove them with 2 spoons and then, holding them with a tea towel, shake the marrows out onto a plate. Set them aside to cool and then chill them in the fridge until solid.

3. Melt the butter in a frying pan and fry the onion and the rice for 1 minute.

4. Pour over the red wine and the stock, and stir in the saffron.

5. Transfer to an ovenproof dish. Cut the marrow into small cubes and place the marrow over the rice. Season with salt and pepper.

6. Cover with a lid and cook in a hot oven for approximately 20 minutes. Serve straight from the oven.

TIME   Preparation takes about 5 minutes, chiling time for the marrow is approximately 30 minutes and cooking time is about 40 minutes.

VARIATION   Reserve half of the marrow at Step 5 and stir it into the cooked risotto.

WATCHPOINT   The volume of liquid should always be 1½ times that of the volume of rice. Water may be substituted for the stock.

☐

OPPOSITE

MILANESE RISOTTO

VEAL IN MARJORAM SAUCE

*A deliciously rich tasting dish. Serve with lots
of crusty bread to mop up the sauce.*

☐ 4 veal escalopes, cut into very thin slices
☐ ½ onion, finely chopped
☐ 2 large mushrooms, cut into very thin slices
☐ 1 clove garlic, chopped ☐ 1 tbsp fresh marjoram
☐ 2 tsps chopped parsley
☐ ¾ cup chicken stock ☐ 2 tbsps olive oil
☐ Flour for dredging ☐ Salt and pepper

1. Season the thin slices of veal with salt and pepper and toss in the flour. Shake off any excess flour.

2. Heat the oil in a frying pan and gently fry the onion, mushrooms and garlic for a few minutes.

3. Add the thin slices of veal, marjoram and parsley. Stir and turn the slices of meat over once.

4. Pour over the stock and cook until it reduces to a thickish sauce. Shake and stir the contents of the pan occasionally.

5. Taste and adjust seasoning and serve hot.

TIME   Preparation takes about 10 minutes and cooking takes approximately 35 minutes.

COOK'S TIP   Make sure you shake off all excess flour from veal, otherwise the coating will be too thick and sticky.

VARIATION   A little butter can be whisked into the sauce to make it richer. Remove the meat at the end of Step 5 and whisk in small knobs of butter. Place the meat back into the sauce before serving.

VARIATION   If you do not have fresh herbs for the recipes, use dried herbs, reducing the amount to between ⅓ and ½.

☐

OPPOSITE

VEAL IN MARJORAM
SAUCE

RICE BALLS

*These meat, cheese and rice balls are a great favorite
with children and adults alike. For more
sophisticated palates, spice them up with herbs.*

Step 5

Step 6

Step 6

□ 1 cup cooked rice (risotto style)
□ ½ cup ground beef   □ 3 slices Mozzarella cheese
□ ½ cup grated Parmesan cheese   □ 1 egg, beaten
□ 1 tsp chopped parsley   □ Breadcrumbs
□ Salt and pepper   □ Oil for deep frying

1. Mix together the rice and ground meat.

2. Stir into the above the parsley, grated Parmesan and the Mozzarella, cut into small cubes.

3. Season well with salt and pepper.

4. Bind together using half of the beaten egg.

5. With slightly moist fingers, shape this mixture into small meatballs.

6. Dip the rice balls in the remaining egg and then roll them in the breadcrumbs.

7. Set the balls aside to rest for 20 minutes.

8. Heat the oil to 300°F and then lower in the rice balls. Remove when golden and crisp. Drain quickly on paper towels and serve as soon as possible.

TIME   Preparation takes about 15 minutes, resting time is at least 20 minutes and, depending on how many batches you make, total cooking time is approximately 10 to 15 minutes.

VARIATION   Add a little finely chopped rosemary to the ground meat

WATCHPOINT   Try to make all the rice balls of an equal size so that they cook through together.

□

OPPOSITE

RICE BALLS

—— SERVES 4 ——

VEAL OLIVES
WITH MUSHROOMS

*Tasty and impressive, these mushroom and shallot stuffed
"olives" are served with a delicious, creamy sauce.*

Step 1

Step 2

Step 2

☐ 4 thin veal escalopes   ☐ 6 large mushrooms
☐ 1 shallot, chopped   ☐ ¼ cup butter
☐ 2 tbsps heavy cream   ☐ 1 cup chicken stock
☐ ½ cup light cream   ☐ 2 tbsps oil
☐ Salt and pepper

1. Trim and wash the mushrooms. Dry them well with a tea towel and chop in a food processor.

2. Melt the butter in a frying pan and gently sauté the shallot and the mushrooms. Season with salt and pepper, allow the water from the mushrooms to evaporate and then stir in the heavy cream. Allow to reduce a little and then set aside to cool.

3. Flatten the escalopes between 2 sheets of plastic wrap, gently beating them with the flat of a large knife.

4. Remove the plastic wrap, season with salt and pepper and then place the cream filling down the center of each escalope.

5. Roll up carefully and secure with kitchen string.

6. Heat the oil and seal the meat rolls on all sides until lightly browned all over.

7. Transfer to a medium oven to finish cooking, turning them over from time to time to ensure even cooking.

8. Add the chicken stock to the remaining cream filling, then beat in the light cream and allow it to reduce somewhat. Check and adjust seasoning and serve poured over the "olives" when they are cooked through.

TIME   Preparation takes about 20 minutes and total cooking time is approximately 25 minutes.

COOK'S TIP   Placing the escalopes between 2 sheets of plastic wrap makes it easier to flatten them.

WATCHPOINT   Stir the mixture continuously throughout Step 2 to prevent it from sticking to the base of the pan.

☐

OPPOSITE

VEAL OLIVES WITH
MUSHROOMS

VEAL WITH MARSALA SAUCE

A smooth, slightly sweet sauce assures the success of this recipe.

Step 1

Step 2

☐ 2lbs shoulder of veal, cut into cubes   ☐ 2 tbsps oil
☐ ¼ cup almond-flavored Marsala
☐ 1 large onion, finely sliced   ☐ 1 sprig rosemary
☐ Salt and pepper

1. Heat the oil and fry the onion and meat until sealed all over and nicely browned.

2. Deglaze the pan with the Marsala and pour over sufficient water to completely cover the meat.

3. Add the rosemary to the pan, season with salt and pepper and simmer gently for 45 minutes.

4. Remove from the heat and serve when the meat is cooked through and the sauce has reduced and thickened.

TIME   Preparation takes about 10 minutes and cooking takes approximately 1 hour.

SERVING IDEA   Serve this dish with sautéed wild mushrooms.

WATCHPOINT   The exact cooking time will depend on the quality of the veal and the size of the cubes; check for doneness and tenderness during cooking and remove from the heat when done.

☐

OPPOSITE

VEAL WITH
MARSALA SAUCE

—— SERVES 4 ——

ROAST PORK FILLET WITH ROSEMARY

An easy dish for when you want to spend time with your guests and not in the kitchen.

Step 2

Step 2

□ 1¾ lb pork fillet   □ Rectangular strip of pork fat
□ 2 cloves garlic, chopped   □ 1 sprig rosemary, chopped
□ ½ tsp coarse sea salt   □ 1 tbsp oil
□ Few leaves tarragon   □ Pepper

---

1. Spread out the fat and sprinkle over the garlic, rosemary, sea salt, pepper and tarragon.

2. Place the fillet in the center of the prepared fat and roll the fat around the meat. Secure with kitchen string.

3. Brush an ovenproof dish with oil, place in the pork fillet and roast in a hot oven for 45 minutes, turning the pork over once, halfway through cooking.

4. Serve either hot or cold, cut into thick slices with the cooking juices spooned over.

TIME   Preparation takes about 15 minutes and cooking takes approximately 45 minutes.

VARIATION   Sprinkle the pork fat with different herbs.

COOK'S TIP   Prepare the meat the day before cooking to allow the herbs and garlic to flavor the meat thoroughly.

□

OPPOSITE

ROAST PORK
FILLET WITH
ROSEMARY

——— SERVES 4 ———

VEAL IN CREAM SAUCE

The delicate taste of veal is complemented by the creamy sauce in this tasty casserole dish.

Step 1

Step 2

Step 3

□ 1⅓ lbs shoulder of veal □ 1 onion, finely sliced
□ ½ tsp marjoram □ 1 tsp lemon juice
□ 1 cup chicken stock □ ½ cup light cream
□ 1 egg yolk □ 3 tbsps olive oil □ Salt and pepper

1. Heat the oil and gently fry the onion for 1 minute.

2. Add the meat to the frying pan and sauté until lightly browned. Tip out any excess fat and pour the contents of the pan into a flameproof casserole.

3. Pour the stock into the casserole and add sufficient water to cover. Sprinkle over the marjoram and stir.

4. Cover and cook for approximately 1 hour and 15 minutes, checking the meat for tenderness and adding water should the level of liquid drop too much.

5. Beat the egg yolk into the cream.

6. Remove the meat from the casserole and keep warm.

7. Over a very gentle heat, whisk the cream mixture into the sauce. Continue whisking over the heat until the sauce thickens. Remove immediately from the heat, stir in the lemon juice, season with salt and pepper, pour over the meat and serve.

TIME   Preparation takes about 10 minutes and cooking takes approximately 1 hour and 25 minutes.

SERVING IDEA   Serve with steamed green beans.

WATCHPOINT   The blending and thickening of the sauce should be done quickly over a very low heat.

□

OPPOSITE

VEAL IN CREAM
SAUCE

MILANESE STYLE OSSO BUCO

*Sliced knuckle of veal cooked in a marvelous tomato
and white wine sauce flavored with garlic and herbs.*

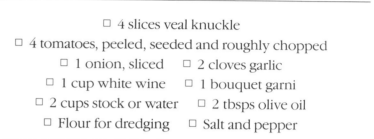

□ 4 slices veal knuckle
□ 4 tomatoes, peeled, seeded and roughly chopped
□ 1 onion, sliced   □ 2 cloves garlic
□ 1 cup white wine   □ 1 bouquet garni
□ 2 cups stock or water   □ 2 tbsps olive oil
□ Flour for dredging   □ Salt and pepper

1. Season the meat with salt and pepper, toss in the flour and then seal in the oil over a high heat.

2. Remove the meat when it is nicely browned and in the same oil fry the onion and garlic for a few minutes.

3. Return the meat to the pan, then deglaze the pan with the wine and allow it to reduce until it has almost all evaporated.

4. Stir in the stock or water, tomatoes and the bouquet garni. Season with salt and pepper.

5. Simmer gently for approximately 1½ hours, checking the level of the liquid and adding water or stock as necessary.

6. Remove the bouquet garni and serve hot.

TIME   Preparation takes about 10 minutes and cooking takes approximately 2 hours.

SERVING IDEA   Serve with pasta spirals lightly tossed in butter.

WATCHPOINT   The cooking time will depend on the thickness of the meat. Add more water and cook longer if the meat is not cooked after 1½ hours.

□

OPPOSITE

MILANESE STYLE
OSSO BUCO

——— SERVES 4 ———

TRUFFLE RISOTTO

Rice, bacon, onion and fresh truffle,
all cooked in a rich chicken stock – delicious!

Step 1

☐ 2 cups rice
☐ 1 thick strip bacon, cut widthwise into strips
☐ 2 medium-sized truffles   ☐ ½ onion, finely chopped
☐ 3 cups chicken stock   ☐ 2 tbsps butter
☐ Salt and pepper

1. Using a small, very sharp knife, cut the truffles into thin slices.

2. Heat the butter gently and add the onion to the pan. Allow the onion to just begin cooking and then stir in the bacon and the rice.

3. Stir well and cook for 1 minute.

4. Add the truffles and pour over the stock. Season with salt and pepper.

5. Transfer to an ovenproof dish and cook, covered, in a hot oven for approximately 20 minutes. Serve immediately on removal from the oven.

TIME   Preparation takes about 8 minutes and total cooking time is approximately 25 minutes.

COOK'S TIP   Stir a little butter into the risotto just before serving.

WATCHPOINT   Fresh truffles, either black or white, give this dish a particularly rich flavor, although the canned variety may be used as an alternative.

☐

OPPOSITE

TRUFFLE RISOTTO

———— SERVES 4-6 ————

BANANA ICE CREAM

A delicious ice cream that is a favorite with children – for adults, add a spoonful of rum!

Step 2

Step 3

Step 3

FOR 4 CUPS EGG CUSTARD

☐ 4 cups milk   ☐ 12 egg yolks   ☐ ½ cup sugar
☐ ½ lb peeled banana   ☐ Few drops lemon juice

1. Prepare the egg custard in the usual way. Whisk the eggs and sugar together until the mixture pales. Bring the milk to the boil and stir in the egg-sugar mixture. Reduce the heat and continue stirring until the mixture thickens. For this recipe use 1 cup of the egg custard, using the remainder for other flavored ice cream.

2. Mash the banana with a fork and add a few drops of lemon juice.

3. Add the banana to the egg custard and blend smooth with a hand mixer.

4. Pour into the bowl of an ice cream maker and set in motion.*

5. Spoon into a container and keep in the freezer until needed.

*If an ice cream maker is not available, pour the mixture into a bowl and place in the freezer until part frozen. Remove from the freezer and whisk. Refreeze and whisk thoroughly until smooth. Pour into a covered container and replace in the freezer until required.

TIME   Preparation takes about 30 minutes and freezing time is approximately 40 minutes to 1 hour (longer if preparing in the freezer).

VARIATION   If you wish to use all the egg custard for the Banana Ice Cream, then increase the amount of bananas used to 2¼ lbs.

WATCHPOINT   It is important to add the lemon juice to the bananas to prevent them from discoloring.

SERVING IDEA   For adults, sprinkle over raisins or golden raisins and a tablespoon of rum.

☐

OPPOSITE

BANANA
ICE CREAM

———— SERVES 4 ————

POACHED PEACHES

*Fresh peaches with Amarena cherries are poached
in white wine for a light, springtime dessert.*

Step 2

Step 3

☐ 6 ripe peaches   ☐ 1 can Amarena cherries (reserve the juice)
☐ 2 tbsps ground almonds   ☐ ½ cup white wine

1. Cut the peaches in half and remove the stones.

2. Place a few cherries in the hollow of each peach half, place them side by side in a small pan and add a spoonful of the reserved cherry juice to the center of each peach.

3. Pour the wine into the bottom of the pan and sprinkle the ground almonds over the peaches.

4. Cook in a moderate oven for approximately 25 minutes, checking the level of the wine from time to time. Serve either hot or chilled.

TIME   Preparation takes about 10 minutes and cooking takes approximately 25 minutes.

VARIATION   Nectarines may be substituted for the peaches if preferred.

COOK'S TIP   The almonds should be golden brown after cooking, if this is not so, place under a hot broiler for 1 minute.

☐

OPPOSITE

POACHED PEACHES

THYME SORBET

*Fresh thyme which is still in flower is used to give a
very delicate flavor to this sorbet, which is
traditionally served between the fish and meat courses.*

Step 2

Step 2

☐ 2 cups water   ☐ ¾ cup sugar
☐ 4 small sprigs fresh thyme in flower

1. Boil together the water and sugar until a reasonably thick syrup
is reached – this will take about 15 minutes boiling.

2. Remove from the heat and add the sprigs of thyme. Remove
the thyme from the syrup after 2 minutes and drain the syrup
through a very fine sieve.

3. Pour the syrup into an ice cream maker and set in motion.*

4. When the sorbet has crystallized spoon into a container and
keep in the freezer until needed.

*If an ice cream maker is not available, pour the strained syrup
into a shallow container and place in the freezer until partly
frozen. Remove from freezer, gently break the mixture up with a
fork, then return to the freezer until needed.

TIME   Preparation time is approximately 30 minutes and
crystallizing the sorbet takes about 30 minutes to 1 hour in an ice
cream maker – longer if using the freezer method.

VARIATION   Use different herbs to flavor this type of sorbet.

WATCHPOINT   Do not allow the thyme to remain in the syrup
for longer than 2 minutes; the flavor is transferred very quickly.

☐

OPPOSITE

THYME SORBET

SERVES 4

SPONGE CAKE WITH ORANGE AND LEMON ZEST

*A sponge cake to serve at tea time,
or with egg custard for dessert.*

Step 1

Step 3

Step 5

□ ⅓ cup sugar   □ ⅓ cup butter, softened at room temperature
□ 2 eggs, separated   □ ⅓ cup all-purpose flour, sifted
□ 4 tbsps cornstarch, sifted   □ 1 tsp baking powder
□ 1 tbsp orange and lemon zest, blanched and drained
□ Pinch of salt   □ Butter for greasing   □ Flour for dredging

1. Whisk the sugar, butter and egg yolks together for a few minutes.

2. Whisk the flour, cornstarch, baking powder and a pinch of salt into the above, adding it little by little and beating continuously.

3. Stir in the orange and lemon zest.

4. Beat the egg whites until very stiff.

5. Gently fold the egg whites into the cake mixture.

6. Grease a cake pan with butter and sprinkle with flour. Pour in the cake mixture and bake in a hot oven for approximately 35 minutes. Serve warm or cold.

TIME   Preparation takes about 25 minutes and baking time is approximately 35 minutes.

COOK'S TIP   Check the cake with a warm skewer after about 25 minutes – if the skewer comes out clean, then the cake is ready. Cooking times vary greatly for different ovens. Keep a note of the timing for future reference.

SERVING IDEA   Should the cake be too dry after a day or two, squeeze over a little orange juice and serve with custard as a dessert.

□

OPPOSITE

SPONGE CAKE
WITH ORANGE
AND LEMON ZEST

───── SERVES 4 ─────

AMARENA ICE CREAM

*Amarena is an Italian variety of
plum-colored cherry that gives
this ice cream its heavenly taste.*

Step 1

Step 2

Step 3

☐ 2 cups milk   ☐ 6 egg yolks   ☐ ½ cup sugar
☐ 4 tbsps canned Amarena cherries, in their juice, roughly chopped

1. Whisk together the egg yolks and the sugar until the mixture whitens.

2. Bring the milk to the boil and whisk it into the egg mixture.

3. Reduce the heat and whisk continuously until the mixture thickens.

4. Remove from the heat and stir in the chopped Amarena cherries and their juice.

5. Pour into the bowl of an ice cream maker and set in motion.*

6. Spoon into a container once the ice cream has crystallized, and keep in the freezer until needed.

*If an ice cream maker is not available, pour the mixture into a bowl and place in the freezer until partly frozen. Remove bowl from freezer and whisk the mixture. Refreeze, whisk thoroughly, and pour into a covered container. Freeze until firm.

TIME   Preparation time is about 30 minutes and freezing time in the machine between 30 minutes and 1 hour – longer if prepared in a freezer.

SERVING IDEA   Chop a few more cherries and sprinkle over the ice cream just before serving.

WATCHPOINT   It is important to whisk rapidly and constantly when the milk is added to the egg mixture, otherwise the eggs will give a curdled look to the mixture.

☐

OPPOSITE

AMARENA
ICE CREAM

————— SERVES 4 —————

HONEY ICE CREAM WITH PINE NUTS

This ice cream, with its flavor of honey and pine nuts, is so good that you will find yourself making it regularly.

Step 1

Step 3

Step 4

☐ 2 cups milk ☐ 6 egg yolks ☐ 2 tbsps honey
☐ 2 tbsps pine nuts

1. Whisk the honey and the egg yolks together for 1 minute.

2. Bring the milk to the boil.

3. Pour the milk over the egg mixture, whisking continuously.

4. Pour this mixture back into the saucepan, add the pine nuts and place over a very low heat, stirring continuously, until the sauce thickens and will coat the back of a spoon.

5. Allow the above to cool and then pour into the bowl of an ice cream maker. Set the machine in motion.*

6. Once the ice cream has 'taken', spoon into a container and keep in the freezer until needed.

*If an ice cream maker is not available, part freeze the mixture in a bowl, whisk until smooth then refreeze. Whisk again and freeze in a covered container until firm.

TIME   Preparation time is approximately 25 minutes and freezing time is between 45 minutes and 1 hour – longer if prepared in the freezer.

VARIATION   Try a variety of different honeys in this ice cream.

WATCHPOINT   Whisk briskly as you pour the milk onto the egg mixture, as the eggs can coagulate quickly with the absence of sugar in this recipe.

☐

OPPOSITE

HONEY ICE CREAM
WITH PINE NUTS

——— SERVES 4 ———

FROZEN ORANGES

A tasty and attractive sorbet
that is served in orange "shells".

Step 1

Step 3

Step 4

☐ Approximately 6 oranges to make 1½ cups orange juice,
☐ ¾ cup water   ☐ ¾ cup sugar

1. Cut the tops off the oranges and remove the pulp with the help of a small spoon, keeping the orange skins whole.

2. Squeeze the juice from the pulp and measure it until you have 1½ cups of freshly squeezed juice – you may require more oranges for this.

3. Mix together the orange juice, water and sugar. Mix well with a whisk and then pour into an ice cream maker. Set the machine in motion.*

4. When the sorbet is crystallized, spoon back into the orange skins and freeze until needed.

*If an ice cream maker is not available, place the mixture in a shallow container and freeze until mushy. Gently break up with a fork, refreeze, spoon into the chilled orange "shells" and serve.

TIME   Preparation takes about 30 minutes and freezing in the ice cream maker approximately 45 minutes – longer if preparing in the freezer.

SERVING IDEA   Serve with crystallized orange peel.

COOK'S TIP   When you have removed the pulp from the oranges, place the skins in the freezer, so that they are very cold when you fill them with the sorbet.

☐

OPPOSITE

FROZEN ORANGES

APPLE FRITTERS

*A simple dessert that is always popular. Either
dredge with sugar or serve with a fresh fruit coulis.*

Step 4

Step 4

Step 5

- □ 2 Golden Delicious apples, peeled,
  cored and cut into small pieces
- □ ½ cup orange juice   □ ¼ cup Marsala
- □ 1⅛ cups all-purpose flour, sifted   □ ¼ tsp baking powder
- □ ¼ cup ground almonds   □ ½ cup milk
- □ 2 egg yolks   □ ¼ cup sugar   □ Oil for deep frying

1. Marinate the apple in the orange juice and the Marsala for 15 minutes.

2. Mix together the flour, baking powder and the ground almonds.

3. Whisk together the sugar and egg yolks until quite white.

4. Beat together the egg mixture and the flour mixture. Stir in the milk and beat really well.

5. Add the flour and egg mixture to the apples in their marinade. Stir gently to blend the ingredients together evenly. Allow to rest for 10 minutes.

6. Heat the oil and gently add spoonfuls of apple and fritter mixture. Allow to cook through and turn golden brown, then remove with a slotted spoon.

7. Drain on paper towels and serve either hot or cold.

TIME   Preparation takes about 15 minutes and cooking takes about 20 minutes, depending on how many batches you cook.

SERVING IDEA   Serve with a fresh fruit coulis (crushed fruit with a little sugar stirred in), or with an egg custard.

WATCHPOINT   The oil should not be too hot, otherwise the apple will not cook in the center of the batter.

□

OPPOSITE

APPLE FRITTERS

ALMOND AND WALNUT MACAROONS

These crunchy little macaroons go well with any of the ice cream recipes, although they are delicious with after-dinner coffee, too.

Step 3

Step 3

Step 5

☐ 1½ cups ground almonds ☐ 1½ cups ground walnuts
☐ 1⅛ cups sugar ☐ 2 egg whites, stiffly beaten
☐ Flour for sifting

1. Mix the walnuts and almonds together thoroughly.

2. Stir the sugar into the ground nut mixture.

3. Gently fold in the beaten egg whites, making sure that all the ingredients are well incorporated.

4. Place this mixture in a pastry bag fitted with a plain tube.

5. Sprinkle a little flour over a baking tray and pipe out the macaroon mixture into small, even-sized macaroons.

6. Bake in a very low oven, 270°F, for approximately 40 minutes.

7. Allow to cool before serving.

TIME Preparation takes about 20 minutes and baking time is approximately 40 minutes.

VARIATION Replace the ground almonds and walnuts with ground hazelnuts.

COOK'S TIP The macaroons are best eaten within a few hours of baking.

☐

OPPOSITE

ALMOND AND WALNUT MACAROONS

SERVES 4

CARAMEL ICE CREAM

*A smooth ice cream with the flavor of toffee,
served with a creamy caramel sauce.*

Step 3

Step 3

Step 5

☐ 3 egg yolks   ☐ ¾ cup sugar   ☐ 1 cup milk
☐ 2 tbsps heavy cream   ☐ ½ cup water

1. Whisk the egg yolks with 2 tbsps sugar until the mixture whitens.

2. Bring the milk to the boil and pour it onto the egg mixture, whisking continuously. Pour into a saucepan and, whisking continuously, continue cooking over a low heat until a thick egg custard is reached. Remove from the heat and set aside.

3. Place the remaining sugar in a small saucepan with 3 tablespoons water and cook over a high heat until a caramel forms.

4. Remove from the heat and stir in the remaining water. Place back over a very low heat, stirring well so that the water is thoroughly mixed into the caramel. Allow to warm through.

5. Mix ¾ of the above caramel into the egg custard. Pour this into the bowl of the ice cream maker and set the machine in motion.*

6. To make the sauce, mix the cream into the remaining ¼ of caramel and stir well.

7. When the ice cream has crystallized, spoon it into a container and keep in the refrigerator until needed. Serve with the caramel sauce poured over.

* If an ice cream maker is not available, pour the caramel-custard mixture into a bowl and place in freezer until part frozen. Remove from the freezer, whisk and refreeze. Whisk thoroughly until smooth, then pour into a covered container and freeze until firm.

TIME   Preparation takes about 15 minutes and 'cooking' time is approximately 15 minutes. Freezing will take between 45 minutes and 1 hour using an ice cream maker – longer if using the freezer method.

SERVING IDEA   Sprinkle over a little chipped semi-sweet chocolate.

WATCHPOINT   Take care when adding the extra water to the caramel as it may spatter.

☐

OPPOSITE

CARAMEL
ICE CREAM

ACACIA BLOOM FRITTERS

These fritters use the flower from the acacia tree, which grows all over Italy and blooms in the month of May. Well worth trying if you can obtain acacia flowers.

Step 3

Step 5

Step 5

☐ 16 acacia flowers ☐ 1⅛ cups all-purpose flour, sifted
☐ 1 tsp salt ☐ ½ cup lager beer ☐ 1 cup warm water
☐ 1 tbsp fruit-flavored alcohol
☐ 1 tbsp butter, melted ☐ 2 egg whites
☐ 1 cup oil ☐ Sugar for dredging

1. Whisk together the flour, salt, beer and warm water.
2. Whisk in the alcohol and melted butter.
3. Beat the egg whites stiffly and fold them gently into the above.
4. Heat the oil in a pan.
5. Dip the acacia flowers into the batter and then fry them in the medium hot oil, turning them until they are golden brown all over.
6. Drain on kitchen paper and dredge with sugar. Serve hot.

TIME   Preparation takes about 20 minutes and cooking takes approximately 10 minutes.

WATCHPOINT   Be very careful when dipping the flowers into the batter and then into the oil, making sure that the flowers do not drop off their stems.

SERVING IDEA   Serve with a fruit sorbet.

☐

OPPOSITE

ACACIA BLOOM
FRITTERS

—— SERVES 4 ——

STRAWBERRY ICE CREAM

This ice cream can be made with the pieces
of fruit left in small chunks, or
mixed smooth with a hand mixer.

Step 1

Step 1

☐ 1 cup egg custard (see Banana Ice Cream recipe)
☐ ¼ cup light cream
☐ 1⅕ cups strawberries, washed and hulled

1. Either chop the strawberries into small pieces and mix them into the egg custard, or add them whole to the custard and blend smooth with a hand mixer.

2. Stir in the cream and pour into the bowl of an ice cream maker. Set the machine in motion.*

3. When the ice cream has 'taken', spoon into a container and keep in the freezer until needed.

*If an ice cream maker is not available, part freeze the mixture in a bowl, whisk and refreeze. Whisk again, pour into a covered container and freeze until firm.

TIME   If you already have some egg custard the preparation takes 5 minutes and freezing time is 45 minutes to 1 hour using the ice cream maker method. If you have to make the custard, an extra 30 minutes will be needed.

SERVING IDEA   Serve with whole strawberries or with a coulis of fresh strawberries and a little sugar.

VARIATION   The mixture may be sieved after Step 1 if you wish to remove the strawberry seeds.

☐

OPPOSITE

STRAWBERRY
ICE CREAM

—— SERVES 4 ——

GNOCCHI WITH PRUNE FILLING

Sweet gnocchi dough is rolled around a prune which has been flavored with sugar and cinnamon.

Step 4

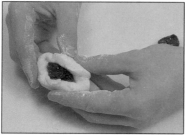

Step 5

Step 6

- □ 24 prunes, stoned
- □ 1lb potatoes, steamed in their skins
- □ 1 cup flour □ ½ egg, beaten □ 1 tbsp milk
- □ ¼ cup butter □ Sugar □ Cinnamon
- □ 3 tbsps Eau de Vie (fruit flavored alcohol)

1. Peel the steamed potatoes and dry them on paper towels. Push the potatoes through a fine sieve.

2. Beat the egg, milk and 2 tbsps butter into the potatoes. Mix really well and then add the flour, beating constantly.

3. When the mixture is really well mixed, form the dough into a ball.

4. Sprinkle a little sugar and cinnamon into each of the stoned prunes.

5. With floured fingers, break off a little gnocchi dough and wrap this around the prune, making sure that the dough is well sealed around the prunes.

6. Bring a large saucepan of water to the boil, add the gnocchi and cook them until they rise to the surface. Remove with a slotted spoon and set aside to dry on a tea towel.

7. Heat the remaining butter in a frying pan and sauté the gnocchi, sprinkling over more sugar and cinnamon to taste. Pour over a little Eau de Vie and serve.

TIME   Preparation takes about 30 minutes and cooking takes approximately 30 minutes.

VARIATION   Fresh plums can be substituted for the prunes. Sprinkle over thin strips of mint to decorate.

COOK'S TIP   Avoid making the gnocchi covering too thick. Serve warm.

□

OPPOSITE

GNOCCHI WITH PRUNE FILLING

SERVES 4

CHOCOLATE ICE CREAM

*A smooth chocolate ice cream made
from a rich egg custard sauce.*

Step 4

Step 4

□ ½ cup sugar   □ 6 egg yolks   □ 2 cups milk
□ 4 tbsps chocolate powder (unsweetened)

1. Whisk the egg yolk and sugar together until the mixture whitens.

2. Bring the milk to boil in a large saucepan.

3. Whisk in the egg mixture, reduce the heat and whisk continuously until the mixture thickens.

4. Once the sauce is thick, remove from the heat and stir in the chocolate powder.

5. Pour the mixture into the bowl of an ice cream maker and set in motion.*

6. Once the ice cream has crystallized it can be spooned into a container and kept in the freezer until needed.

*If an ice cream maker is not available, pour the mixture into a bowl and place in the freezer until mushy. Remove bowl from freezer and whisk the mixture. Refreeze, whisk thoroughly, pour into a covered container and freeze until firm.

TIME   Preparation takes 30 minutes, crystallizing the ice cream, depending on the machine used, will take between 30 minutes and 1 hour – longer if preparing in the freezer

SERVING IDEA   Serve with chips of white and semi-sweet chocolate.

COOK'S TIP   Use plain, unsweetened chocolate powder for this ice cream.

□

OPPOSITE

CHOCOLATE
ICE CREAM

---- SERVES 4 ----

PRUNE ICE CREAM

A simple-to-make, rich-tasting ice cream.

Step 2

Step 3

☐ 1 cup egg custard (see Banana Ice Cream recipe)
☐ 10 prunes, stoned   ☐ 1 squeeze lemon juice

1. Process the prunes with the lemon juice in a food processor. The prunes will form a thick dark paste.

2. Put this prune paste in a large bowl and pour over the egg custard.

3. Blend with a hand mixer until quite smooth.

4. Pour into the bowl of an ice cream maker and set the machine in motion.*

5. Once the ice cream has 'taken', spoon into a container and keep in the freezer until needed.

* If an ice cream maker is not available, part freeze the mixture, whisk and refreeze. Whisk the mixture again until smooth and creamy, then pour into a covered container and freeze until firm.

TIME   Preparation, if you already have the egg custard, will take about 8 minutes, and freezing time approximately 45 minutes to 1 hour using the ice cream maker – longer if preparing in a freezer.

SERVING IDEA   Serve with prunes which have been soaked in a fruit alcohol. Place small scoops of ice cream on the prunes and pour over the marinade alcohol.

COOK'S TIP   Ice cream should ideally be kept at 10°F, but as most freezers work a few degrees below this temperature, it is advisable to remove the ice cream from the freezer 10 minutes before serving.

Copyright © Frédéric Lebain

☐

OPPOSITE

PRUNE ICE CREAM

—— SERVES 4 ——

RHUBARB SORBET

A very refreshing sorbet. Serve as a light dessert after a particularly rich meal.

Step 1

Step 1

☐ 1½ cups water   ☐ ⅞ cup sugar   ☐ 1lb rhubarb

1. Peel the rhubarb and cut the stalks into small pieces.
2. Mix together in a saucepan the water, sugar and rhubarb.
3. Bring to the boil and cook for 5 minutes.
4. Blend smooth with a hand mixer and pour into the bowl of an ice cream maker. Set the machine in motion and remove when the sorbet is crystalized. Spoon into a container and keep in the freezer until needed.

*If an ice cream maker is not available, part freeze the mixture in a shallow container, break up gently with a fork and then pour into a covered container and freeze until needed.

TIME   Preparation takes about 10 minutes and freezing in the ice cream maker takes approximately 40 minutes.

SERVING IDEA   Serve on a bed of finely sliced rhubarb which has been cooked for 2 minutes in very little water and sweetened to your liking. Allow the sorbet to soften somewhat before serving.

WATCHPOINT   Stop the ice cream maker and spoon the sorbet into a container when it has crystalized. The mixture should be neither too hard not too soft.

☐

OPPOSITE

RHUBARB SORBET